PROCESS
ALCHEMY

PROCESS ALCHEMY

Using Employee-Driven Solutions
To Achieve Operational Excellence

MARIBEL ARANGO TOPF

INDIE BOOKS
INTERNATIONAL

PROCESS ALCHEMY

Contents

Preface

This is the book I needed ten years ago, but it simply did not exist. After completing an intensive six-month black belt Lean Six Sigma course during a career transition at my company, I sought materials offering practical, real-world applications of my newfound knowledge. I scoured bookshelves, sought mentors, and yearned for concrete examples, insider insights, and the pitfalls to avoid.

Over the years, fellow practitioners have urged me to share this knowledge. While manufacturing remains important, the scarcity of resources providing real-life examples of continuous improvement practices in an office setting became apparent. Valuable information often came at a hefty price, locked behind the doors of expensive conferences or sporadic webinars. Alternative sources of examples are suspect, as white papers and industry conferences transformed into platforms for companies pushing their services or software "solutions" to CI practitioners.

Though practitioners were not in short supply, coaxing them to share their stories proved challenging. While willing to assist others, most wanted to uphold a positive company image while revealing internal challenges to strangers. This book delves into the overlooked areas seldom discussed in Lean Six Sigma training.

Continuous improvement professionals often face impossible requests, akin to navigating a battlefield with scars acquired from unforeseen lessons in human psychology and hidden processes. These pages unfold an unreserved narrative, offering an unfiltered glimpse into my journey as a continuous improvement practitioner, detailing the challenges, triumphs, and inevitable mishaps encountered while creating an operational excellence culture in the distinct dynamics of an office environment.

Like the Navy SEALs or any elite military group, the goal of any program is to develop effective teams empowered to make decisions at critical moments. Like winning in the stock market, operational excellence concepts are easy to understand. Buy low and sell high. The concept is simple, but execution is not.

Like all newly minted continuous improvement (CI) practitioners, I felt I understood the challenges. Armed with Post-it notes, diagrams, and a wealth of process-mapping wisdom, I confidently stepped into the arena, only to face a harsh reality. Everyone teaches you the happy path to problem-solving and change management. No one covers the reality of complex issues, limited resources, strong egos, senior management teams, personality challenges, and the dark side of technology.

I became Deanna Troi from *Star Trek: The Next Generation*. Part empath, part counselor, entrusted with hundreds of honest conversations filled with frustrations and apprehension by management and employees. Prepare to delve into the minds of the human engines that propel our businesses forward. Experience a unique vantage point into my decade-long journey spanning two companies and eight global facilities while interacting with thousands of employees over the years. Through these interactions, I amassed a collection of best practices and wisdom gleaned from overseeing over 10,000 small and large projects.

I've collaborated closely with divisional presidents and CI managers, leading the charge in cultural transformation. Discover how to construct an organization capable of consistently recognizing and solving current and anticipated problems. Witness the transformation when teams shift from perpetual excuses to continuous problem-solving. Build the synergy needed to take your teams from mundane tasks to peak performance. These are the techniques I have found invaluable to break free from the cycle of repeatedly *solving* the same problem. Dive into the core principles of Lean Six Sigma fundamentals originally honed on the manufacturing floor and learn how to apply them in an office setting. Calibrate teams and data the way you would a machine in a cell.

PART ONE

Why A Culture Of Operational Excellence Matters

CHAPTER 1

Building An Operational Excellence Road Map

Operational excellence helps you retain relevancy in a rapidly changing world. It requires an organization to become process and data-driven, viewing every task and decision as a process. It is resisting the temptation to rely on temporary fixes and workarounds and instead establishing a framework that empowers employees to make meaningful contributions to the organization.

Any employee can put the organization at risk, harm its reputation, or trigger unnecessary crises. This is why every employee should actively contribute to the organization's success. It's crucial for businesses to continuously innovate, tackle challenges, foster a culture of learning, and manage expenses effectively. If nothing changes, what do you think will?

The Role Of Leadership In Operational Excellence

Since the beginning, I have struggled with what leadership's role is in operational excellence. A function of the management team should be to inspire employees to think beyond boundaries. What is considered impossible that, if achieved, could revolutionize your approach? My journey has exposed me to various companies, within and outside of my organization, each adopting different methodologies—be it top-down, bottom-up, a combination of both, or a system with limited management involvement. I have mixed feelings about the best method, as every company boasts distinct work styles and unique cultures. In both companies I worked for, most teams were bottom-up. Leadership defined *what* had to be done while removing obstacles when necessary.

Employees define *how* it will be done. As a company's greatest asset, they should be granted autonomy to organize themselves into roles that best align with the established strategic goals. Relying solely on management for every decision implies a limiting belief that only they possess the capacity for innovative ideas and discoveries. Empowering employees to take the initiative allows the organization to tap into a wealth of creativity and expertise, fostering a more dynamic and adaptive workplace. They need to learn the art of prioritization and an infrastructure and process to identify all resources available, from skill sets to technology needed to overcome obstacles.

In my observation from top-down teams, rigid command and control approaches compelled management to micromanage every decision. This led to delayed responses and a slower learning curve that impacted productivity and performance. Effective management needs visibility into every facet of the organization to enable timely and critical decisions. This requires the collective vigilance of all employees, as their keen eyes are essential in spotting both issues and opportunities.

Traditional management models often rely on fixed, linear processes and hierarchies. However, dynamic systems theory recognizes businesses as complex, adaptive systems where multiple variables interact unpredictably. Nature provides us with fascinating examples of dynamic systems theory at work, such as ants and bees, where efficiency thrives through independent work guided by straightforward rules and signaling methods. Bottlenecks are avoided by not having one organism attempting to organize or make group decisions. Instead, many hive-style insects and animals employ a range of signals to communicate instructions swiftly. In modern project management, especially in agile methodologies and change management, you can see how dynamic systems theory principles are applied in business. Both processes use an iterative approach to work with constant feedback loops, enabling teams to promptly respond to challenges and opportunities. A dynamic approach to dealing with the inherent complexities of organizational change involves continuous feedback, adaptation, and learning.

In a world where resources are scarce, throwing money at the problem discourages creativity and promotes wasteful thinking. Working with our teams taught me valuable lessons:

- **Freedom Fuels Innovation:** Teams thrive when given the freedom and empowerment to tackle issues with minimal bureaucracy—without excessive approvals or documentation.

- **Recognition Drives Effort:** Employees work harder when their ideas and efforts are consistently acknowledged, even in small gestures. Even if not implemented, recognizing and evaluating their ideas is crucial for sustaining their engagement.

- **Fostering Culture Through Storytelling:** Stories about managers' behavior, how failures were managed, and how credit was distributed all shape and reinforce the organizational culture. These narratives become integral parts of how culture is perceived and upheld.

Shaping Operational Excellence Through Strategic Hiring Practices

In the realm of operational excellence, hiring practices play a pivotal role in defining the success trajectory of any organization. The selection and integration of new talent are not mere administrative tasks but strategic moves that can either bolster or hinder operational efficiency, innovation, and overall performance.

High employee turnover rates can signal deeper issues within a company, such as burnout, a toxic manager or culture, or various underlying root causes. The impact of turnover will be displayed in quality, workplace culture, higher hiring and training costs, and disruption to team dynamics and project continuity.

Navigating hiring practices requires a delicate balance between harnessing the strengths of seasoned professionals and embracing the fresh perspectives brought by newer generations. Seasoned employees, often with a wealth of experience, contribute qualities such as consistency, a reliable work ethic, and meticulous attention to project details, significantly enhancing the success of projects.

On the flip side, newer generations inject vitality into the workforce by offering innovative technological solutions, a contemporary outlook, and an infectious enthusiasm for their roles. Thus, a forward-looking hiring strategy must strike a harmonious balance between the invaluable strengths of experienced professionals and the innovative contributions of the newer workforce to ensure sustained success and growth.

The most effective approach acknowledges and integrates the unique values of both groups. However, a common pitfall is allowing established team members to wield excessive influence over work processes, fostering resistance to change, particularly as leadership ages. When the prevailing sentiment becomes, "we'll make a change when _____ retires," it hinders progress. This reluctance to adapt can result in career stagnation for newer generations, who crave a dynamic and evolving work culture.

In addition to bringing in talent and skill sets through external hires, foster a proactive approach within your organization to become a learning-oriented entity. Allocate a portion of your team to continuously enhance their skills or engage in activities such as networking, which exposes them to diverse ideas and viewpoints. Implement a structured process for teams to share their learning experiences, exchange best practices, and motivate one another to delve deeper into areas that can benefit both team members and the organization as a whole.

CHAPTER 2

The Role Of Daily Work In Operational Excellence

When I took over the CI role, the company's president tasked me with ingraining it within our culture, moving beyond mere stand-alone Kaizen events. I entered a work environment where continuous improvement was viewed as an extra burden, something perceived as stealing time from their work or posing a threat to job security. Step one became integrating continuous improvement into their daily tasks through the following initiatives:

- Four hours of CI training annually

- Enhancing their skill set or improving at least one work process each year

- Collaborating on one team project

Continuous improvement needs to evolve into a guiding principle: aiming to enhance your daily tasks every day. It's vital for employees to approach their work with a fresh perspective, constantly seeking opportunities for minor enhancements every day. Every transaction, customer interaction, and business process serves as a foundation for improvement. Starting small, such as encouraging employees to tidy up desks, network folders, and emails, can have a cumulative impact throughout the organization, resulting in heightened engagement and energy levels.

Waiting to address processes only when they break is a common error. Similar to machines on a manufacturing floor, process design, and infrastructure demand regular maintenance and feedback loops for sustained effectiveness. Open conversations with employees about their tasks, encouraging them to share frustrations with existing processes. Identifying areas for improvement while the process is still functional is key to promoting a proactive approach to enhancement.

For continuous improvement (CI) professionals, addressing these concerns with employees' managers is crucial, as many individuals may hesitate to raise such issues themselves. If you are a manager, ensure you use encouraging language that emphasizes solutions, steering clear of any words that could be interpreted as assigning blame.

Transforming the culture also means instilling a practice where management consistently poses questions and encourages employees to seek improvements on their own proactively. "Let's do a CI to fix this" emerged as a straightforward technique to kick-start any improvement project.

Large improvement projects can quickly become overwhelming and should be divided by the amount of effort needed to be completed in a month. These could be handled as multiday improvement events with a facilitator or as a project with a series of team meetings. Teams need to be working on at least one improvement project at all times.

Quality Cost = Prevention Cost + Appraisal Cost + Failure Cost[1]

The formula above underscores the role of daily work in driving improvement and innovation. Prevention encompasses activities aimed at embedding quality into the product creation or service execution process. Appraisal covers all costs related to inspection or testing. The introduction of complexity introduces numerous hidden costs, including extra steps, workarounds, and additional personnel or processes. Over time, these hidden costs manifest as a slowdown in tasks and increased issues stemming from unforeseen scenarios. Repeated failures not only jeopardize an organization's reputation but also have a cascading effect on sales, employee retention, stock performance, and other critical aspects.

Let's not overlook the often-underestimated expense of maintenance, which tends to be one of the costliest aspects with limited visibility. Maintenance costs encompass all the expenditures necessary to maintain physical or digital assets in optimal working condition. Upon closer consideration, nearly every acquisition involves some form of maintenance cost, covering labor, spare parts, and even energy consumption. Moreover, costs extend beyond financial considerations.

Upgrades or updates may entail a learning curve, consuming time in planning for maintenance, or the downtime resulting from either conducting the maintenance or the repercussions of neglecting it and facing an inevitable breakdown. It's imperative to recognize and factor in these multifaceted costs to ensure a comprehensive understanding of the true investment associated with any asset or system. Six Sigma methodology has levels that determine the probability that an error or defect will occur. A company operating at about 3.5 sigma spends about twenty percent of its costs on maintenance and rectifying defects. This is because they are at about 97.7 percent efficiency, creating nearly 22,700 mistakes per million opportunities.

In contrast, a company running at six sigma generates 3.4 mistakes per million opportunities. With so few errors, the need for additional rework is drastically reduced, resulting in less than 5 percent of time and money being spent on quality.[2] While attaining this level of excellence comes with a price tag, many organizations tend to overlook the expenses associated with a lack of maintenance. Once these costs are considered, investing in upgrading systems or processes can substantially decrease long-term expenses and enable employees to engage in more productive tasks.

Employee-related process failures typically fall into these two categories:

- Correct methods were not taught accurately or assessed for proficient execution.

- Correct methods are understood but not implemented due to careless mistakes, insufficient skills, or time constraints (a shortened deadline).

In a culture of process excellence, establishing a framework for interdepartmental collaboration, transparency, and process visibility becomes essential. A robust infrastructure sets the stage for identifying and eliminating obstacles, fostering an environment where excuses hold no ground. It encourages a proactive approach to process innovation, even amidst competing priorities and busy schedules.

A hallmark of an excellent culture is when employees recognize the distinction between improvement and change. Change involves altering something, whether it's the color, shape, or a complete redesign, and while change may lead to improvement, it's not a guaranteed outcome. Similarly, investing significant time and effort in altering a process doesn't automatically translate to improvement; improvement must be measurable in some way.

When employees tackle a challenge, my first step is encouraging them to delve into why that specific issue is essential. As a practitioner, I consistently push them to articulate the logic behind investing time and resources in these improvements. Questions such as, "What makes this effort worthwhile? What benefits do you expect to achieve?" are crucial. I've observed that employees often find it challenging to express the rationale behind their proposed changes. It's imperative for them to discern early in the process whether they're initiating a change to the process or genuinely improving it. Misjudging this distinction could lead to the wastage of valuable resources.

Extracting Lessons From Failure

In organizations valuing problem-solving, innovation, and engaged employees, failure is embraced as an inherent aspect of the learning journey. Teams openly discuss both successes and failures, fostering confidence and granting access to the essential resources for finding solutions.

Conversely, in environments where failure is not tolerated, secrecy and a lack of transparency tend to characterize the culture. Keeping vital information hidden results in ill-informed decisions and choices made with incomplete data. Stories shared within the organization should inspire and captivate employees while conveying valuable lessons about the company's culture and values.

One of the most memorable moments in my career was the day a meeting was called to discuss a significant issue with our flagship product. At that time, we didn't have a redundant copy of our application to minimize interruptions, and the product had been intermittently down for several days. The impact on the customer and our client services increased with every moment of product instability. The tension in the room was palpable, and the body language of the person trying to explain the situation was a masterclass in "I'd rather be anywhere else." Everyone was eerily quiet as they awaited the reaction of the senior manager. The pivotal moment our company's culture took a turn in the right direction came when I heard his response.

"What did we learn?"

Four simple words completely transformed the energy in the room. It allowed the team to fully analyze the missteps and proactively engage in discussions leading toward a solution. Most importantly, valuable time wasn't squandered on assigning blame or seeking punishment. Assume employees tried their best with the resources at hand, so falling short is seen as part of the learning process, with the rest of the team pitching in to assist. Issues are rarely caused deliberately or with malicious intent. When an engineer at Pixar accidentally deleted the only working copy of

Toy Story 2, the entire team immediately launched into action in trying to find a recovery solution. As the CEO tells the story, the team focused on three items after the accident: restoring the film, fixing the backup systems, and installing precautionary restrictions so the incident could not occur again. There was no need or desire to assign blame.[3]

Language plays a defining role in establishing psychological safety and fostering a culture of operational excellence. How a company addresses failures is a key determinant of its culture. When discussing failure, there is a huge difference between saying, "Mark broke it," and "The process is broken." The former implies Mark made a mistake, but if the process itself is flawed, anyone following it is set up for failure. It's crucial to assume the process is faulty initially, allowing everyone, including Mark, to openly discuss observed issues. The choice of words used to describe a flawed process can motivate staff to promptly and proactively seek solutions rather than creating a barrier to honesty and cooperation.

Our perception of the world often leads us to either exaggerate problems or downplay significant issues to escape harsh realities. Data is easily taken out of context. We witness how the media and algorithms can manipulate data to influence our thinking. Numerous cognitive biases lead us to question even our own observations.

Understanding the challenge can help us create more effective frameworks. Maintaining the discipline to be process-driven over gut reactions enables teams to pause and evaluate solutions carefully. It's essential to establish environments where differing opinions are accepted, fostering openness to diverse interpretations of data.

The Role Of Human Psychology In Operational Excellence

One of the most significant challenges I've encountered with many teams is the perceived threat my presence seemed to pose. It's a recurring theme—the instinct to prove me wrong, irrespective of the subject matter. You've likely come across various versions of this scenario. Talk to someone trying to lose weight, and they will tell you they are doing *everything* right. They're exercising, monitoring their caloric intake, and even vehemently defending their approach when you point out that something evidently isn't working or being done effectively if they're not losing weight. It's human nature to regard the messenger as the problem itself.

Any CI practitioner or manager tasked to address an issue has undoubtedly encountered these familiar responses:

"We've exhausted all options."

"I've got it under control."

So, let's think of it from the perspective of uncovering the root cause. Why would people attack the messenger?

One of the core principles drawn from Daniel Kahneman's research is the law of least effort. Both humans and machines instinctively opt for the path of least resistance or effort. But continuous improvement projects demand effort: the analysis, the search for solutions, and the eventual implementation.[4] How many employees genuinely welcome the prospect of additional work? Even if their existing workflow is inefficient and challenging, the idea of change might feel daunting.

Upholding discipline and adherence to processes requires significant effort. Recognizing fundamental human psychology is pivotal in crafting a program that aligns with employees' inherent tendencies. Assume people will skip steps or struggle to recall them. Avoid overloading employees with unnecessary tasks. Design processes that effortlessly align with their existing workflow, promoting a more natural and successful implementation. Borrowing from Nudge Theory, we know people can't be forced to change their behavior. Instead, by presenting options that make desired behaviors more appealing, we can shape and influence change effectively.[5]

Studies show that achieving complete objectivity and being entirely unbiased is incredibly difficult, even with the best intentions. We tend to depend on past experiences, pattern recognition, and existing knowledge to solve problems, often without fully investigating the root cause. This underscores the importance of cultivating a company culture that offers a framework to encourage the emergence and exploration of others' ideas. Engaging a variety of perspectives in the process is essential. This inclusivity brings forth diverse viewpoints, steering the search for solutions in the right direction rather than simply opting for the fastest route.

Lean and Six Sigma methodology offers a structured problem-solving approach that compels us not to skip essential steps or rush to premature conclusions. These methodologies counteract the automatic urge to provide immediate solutions, encouraging a pause for reflection and questioning initial assumptions.

Anticipate the Dunning-Kruger effect during the operational excellence journey. This is the cognitive bias in which unskilled people make poor decisions or reach wrong conclusions because their incompetence renders them unable to recognize their mistakes. The frightening element is that many who display this bias will speak confidently, creating a false impression of superiority or intelligence. Ironically, those truly capable are likely to question their ideas more and create an illusion of incompetence. Genuine intelligence is revealed through the awareness of the vast realms of knowledge that remain unexplored.

----------------------------▽----------------------------

Anticipate the Dunning-Kruger effect during the operational excellence journey. This is the cognitive bias in which unskilled people make poor decisions or reach wrong conclusions because their incompetence renders them unable to recognize their mistakes.

----------------------------△----------------------------

In conclusion:

- Integrate continuous improvement into daily tasks.

- Promote a culture of learning from failures. Create an environment where issues can be openly and proactively discussed on a regular basis.

- Resist the instinctive tendency to reward firefighting and instead praise stability and structure.

- Reinforce the reliance on tested methodologies and tread carefully with untested technology or techniques. Refrain from rewarding extroversion and confidence over data. Teams and employees must feel comfortable navigating the uncertainty created by a constantly changing world.

CHAPTER 3

How Common Misperceptions Hinder Progress

I n my experience, having reviewed and managed close to 5,000 team projects and over 8,000 small personal employee improvements (sometimes referred to as 2 Second Lean[6]), there are several misconceptions I have discovered:

Root-cause issues vary widely. Actually they don't. In reviewing the root cause of hundreds of projects (large and small), failures can be traced back to a breakdown in communication at a critical juncture in the process:

- A misunderstanding in communication, including misinterpretation of words or requests.

- Lack of agreement among team members on their roles and responsibilities.

- Miscommunication due to too many ways of distributing information (phone, text, chat, in-person, meeting, etc.)

More management is needed to drive transformation. You may think so, but no. They must set guidelines and objectives, but teams must be empowered to do the work. Consider this:

- Each additional supervisor results in an increase in meetings and content requests.

- Each manager introduces about 1.5 full-time equivalent employees' worth of unnecessary work to their team.[7]

- In short, more layers of management are likely to lead to higher overhead and a slowdown in work.

The CI practitioner needs to be a subject matter expert. This is a distraction. When the consultant or practitioner is a subject matter expert, they tend to impose their own perspectives. A genuine CI practitioner remains independent of any specific department. The role of the facilitator is to bring out all the creativity and insights from the team. A CI practitioner focuses on observing body language, gathering information, fostering alignment, and ensuring the team's productivity.

A CI practitioner cannot manage multiple projects. This is true when the CI practitioner does the bulk of the work instead of the team. A CI practitioner is a resource, not the lead. Teams are responsible for 95 percent of the work. The CI practitioner facilitates important process-gathering meetings, acts as a mediator, aids in creating decision-making rules, and fulfills similar supportive roles.

Multitasking is a good thing. The greatest killer of organizational productivity is multitasking at all levels. The continuous shifting of attention among multiple priorities only contributes to significant delays in decision-making and execution. There are many reasons for this:

- When a task is interrupted midstream, time is required to refamiliarize yourself with the work and reset to where they were in the process. Often, reworking will be involved.

- It's easy to lose sight of the overall project timeline by focusing too much on completing a task.

- Multitasking causes each task to be completed later than initially expected. The cumulative effect across teams can lead to substantial delays.

- To compensate for multitasking, teams will overestimate the time needed for tasks.

- Multitasking is often exacerbated by multiple managers vying for priority over limited resources, leading to constant project interruption. Instead of allocating needed time to complete a project, individuals are pulled in various directions, often leading to lower-quality work.

- Constantly shifting priorities leads to higher stress levels and burnout across individuals.

- Projects often start too early with a limited understanding of requirements and resources, causing them to halt when resources are unavailable. It's best not to start a project until there is enough time, money, and skill set to dedicate to a speedy completion.

Data gathering is straightforward. Right now, one of our greatest challenges is the amount of data collected. There's a common misconception that merely connecting the dots will lead to profound insights. In my experience, some of the best data gathering comes from personal observation, real-time manual collection, and auditing of data acquisition processes. Allow me to illustrate this with three anecdotes:

- My first experience with database challenges came early in my career. Our phone system was not integrated with the customer relationship management (CRM) system, making connecting call reasons with their respective durations difficult. While the lack of system integration explained this challenge, a more concerning revelation emerged. The same issue was described in at least ten different ways within the CRM system due to an abundance of drop-down choices. This diversity made it exceptionally challenging to identify the issue's impact accurately. My discovery prompted implementing a formal process to assess and streamline the usage of drop-down options. I will delve into the technique we employed later in this book.

- I vividly remember hearing a fellow practitioner's account of tackling a "quality" problem at their manufacturing plant. The product's quality testing had significantly deteriorated, and they struggled to pinpoint the root cause. Upon closer inspection, a crucial insight emerged. The quality tester had been stationed in the middle of the floor for employees' convenience in submitting samples for testing. This central location, however, created two significant issues that were observed firsthand. Firstly, the central spot led to excessive socializing, causing distractions. Secondly, the vibration from other equipment in the area affected the machines used for testing the samples. Once the tester and equipment were relocated to a corner of the plant, the product's quality skyrocketed from the low eighties to the high nineties practically overnight.

• On numerous occasions, I've encountered situations where outdated business rules or newly introduced software systems generate data that can no longer be relied upon. The resulting discrepancies have created unreliable inventory counts, needless investments in hardware to fix non-existent issues, implementation of unnecessary workarounds, and crucial problems being overlooked.

Shaping Company Culture: The Impact Of Data, Information And Technology

Having spent nearly two decades within the organization, I've had the opportunity to observe the remarkable and swift technological advancements and their influence on both the organization and its employees. I've noticed recurring mistakes and wishful thinking across various teams and management choices throughout this period.

It's time to think of data and technology differently. Neglecting to establish clear strategies for technology, data, and information leads to silos, miscommunication, mistakes, and overall confusion. The same principles can be employed by treating data and technology like products. Design all the elements in data and technology stacks and improve upon them like any product or process.

Many sophisticated products and services have come to market to help companies translate information into meaningful data. In the past, this meant acquiring competitive data from public sources or using market research firms to run surveys and gather information. The good news is that normal business software such as CRM (Customer Relationship Management systems) and ERP (Enterprise Resource Planning) systems enable us to accumulate a wealth of information without much effort.

Regrettably, the majority of these products merely structure data into "data cubes" or relational databases, preparing data for analysis without inherently providing value. Such software often comes with generic reports and statistical tools yet lacks an adequate method for handling diverse types of data, such as emails or varying forms of customer contact.

Data can turn insights into informed decisions in the hands of the right decision-makers. A competitive advantage is easily achieved by seamlessly structuring data and information flow throughout the organization. Data should flexibly adapt to business changes, tapping into the potential of employee-driven innovation rather than dictating their methods.

Technology is a tool and a resource; it should not drive the business. Just as the shape of a hammer or screwdriver doesn't dictate the blueprints of a building, our processes, and innovations shouldn't be confined by tool limitations. Instead of adjusting our ideas to fit within these constraints, we should choose tools that enable us to fully explore and execute innovative concepts. Technology is dynamic, yet we often treat it as static, missing out on its full potential.

All technology requires maintenance and upkeep. When selecting a software solution, things often overlooked are password and licensing management, frequency and disruption of upgrades, customization costs, and how well it will integrate with existing systems. When selecting software and hardware solutions, choosing options that offer long-term flexibility and adaptability is crucial. What seems cutting-edge today can quickly transform into a legacy challenge. Features and solutions promised by vendors almost always fall short of expectations. Opting for solutions covering 90 percent of our needs is tempting. The final 10 percent is what distinguishes a successful implementation from a costly failure in both time and money. To illustrate, humans and chimpanzees share up to 99 percent of similar DNA, yet the remaining 1 percent accounts for significant differences. I've witnessed numerous expensive software implementations abandoned after years of attempting to address the final requirements they couldn't successfully meet.

---▽---

Opting for solutions covering 90 percent of our needs is tempting. The final 10 percent is what distinguishes a successful implementation from a costly failure in both time and money.

---△---

Don't be deceived into thinking that the journey to operational excellence requires expensive consultants or an intimidating initial process. It's likely you already possess all the necessary tools at your disposal. In summary:

- Designate someone within your organization as a CI coordinator. They don't need to be a subject matter expert initially; they can learn to become a process expert over time.

- Concentrate on understanding how communication and data flow throughout the organization. This is crucial for enhancing visibility into processes. Identifying gaps or inefficient handoffs will significantly contribute to achieving quick, short-term victories.

- Minimize multi-tasking to increase the speed of work.

- Understand the selection and utilization of data and technology. Understanding how information is gathered and used will assist you in creating a long-term strategy.

PART TWO

Twenty-Five Insights For Establishing And Sustaining Excellence

CHAPTER 4

The Culture

1 The Role Of A CI Professional

There are generally three approaches when a company decides to embark on its operational excellence journey:

- Engage an independent consultant or consulting company to tackle a specific project or provide train-the-trainer.

- Employ a CI facilitator to establish or support an organizational culture of operational excellence.

- Enroll associates in Lean Six Sigma training to understand the fundamentals even without a concrete strategy or plan in place.

The journey begins with an in-depth understanding of the organization's significant challenges and the ultimate goal behind implementing a program. Of course, short-term and long-term goals will require a combination of strategies. You must address urgent issues with fast tactical solutions while developing a long-term sustainable culture.

Bringing in an independent consultant to tackle one or two major projects is a common introduction to process excellence. With a well-defined scope, this approach often yields quick wins. However, this is typically expensive, and the gains may not be sustained over the long-term. Since the consultant manages the project, employee engagement is limited. Projects often lack continuity after the consultant's departure. A good consultant not only manages the project but also trains and coaches staff. Consultants who are solely focused on project management without imparting knowledge should be discouraged.

Bringing a continuous improvement (CI) professional on board marks the start of the cultural transformation journey. These professionals are typically within the human resources (HR), operations, and finance departments. While there is no pre-defined department for CI professionals, one crucial factor is their access to individuals with significant decision-making authority. Their role is not to take sole ownership of identified issues but to aid teams in elevating concerns to the appropriate management level. Ambiguities like "management wouldn't approve" or "management wouldn't invest" shouldn't serve as shields for employees; transparency and accountability are paramount. If the CI professional isn't situated strategically within the senior management team or is confined to reporting positive news, they risk becoming akin to another consultant, spending valuable time attempting to establish influential relationships instead of driving tangible solutions forward.

––––––––––––––––––––– ▽ –––––––––––––––––––

If the CI professional isn't situated strategically within the senior management team or is confined to reporting positive news, they risk becoming akin to another consultant, spending valuable time attempting to establish influential relationships instead of driving tangible solutions forward.

––––––––––––––––––––– △ –––––––––––––––––––

Furthermore, it's crucial for the CI professional to be actively involved in meetings that offer real-time insights into different aspects of the organization. This encompasses stand-up sessions with project or product management, senior management staff meetings, relevant HR discussions, and more. The broader their exposure, the quicker they can establish connections across diverse groups within the organization.

The CI professional plays a pivotal role in establishing an effective process for operational excellence. Once a robust program is in place, the process autonomously drives initiatives, reducing the necessity for the CI professional to continually champion projects forward and allowing teams to take more initiative.

② Understanding The Pitfalls Of Third-Party Support

After twenty-five years of seeing the success rate of third-party business providers, I have concluded that an independent consultant or third-party company cannot offer support without significant internal resources. Ironically, most professional support initiatives were initiated due to a lack of internal resources or expertise to complete a project. Management often expects external expertise to compensate for the time and effort internal resources lack in conducting the necessary process maps and project requirements necessary for success. In the end, internal resources find themselves compensating for third-party consultants who lack insight into the company's institutional knowledge.

Third-party business partners encounter the same hurdles as regular companies: employee turnover, knowledge loss, and time lost due to steep learning curves. When key employees depart and new staff members must be onboarded, it often results in delayed delivery times, higher costs, and budget overruns. Only one consulting company I have encountered stands out. They consistently assign paired project managers and developers to every project, ensuring redundancy and uninterrupted workflow even in the event of employee departure. Most companies don't do this due to the additional costs incurred to ensure client satisfaction.

Internal resources oversee and manage third-party work, negating many benefits. So not only are you paying the third-party company, you are robbing internal resources of the time they were supposed to gain from the additional assistance. Hiring freelancers is a better option than a third-party consulting company. There is less overhead, and due to the direct relationship, they are more invested in the company, leading to a higher likelihood of long-term commitment and learning.

There is less overhead, and due to the direct relationship, they are more invested in the company, leading to a higher likelihood of long-term commitment and learning.

It's important to acknowledge that independent consultants are seen as outsiders to the organization and are seldom embraced as long-term team members. They are not positioned to influence the crucial elements necessary to empower employees effectively to bring their talent and creativity to their roles as part of the culture. Once the team understands the process of doing projects themselves, employees can scale continuous improvement practices to large or small projects.

If a consulting company is required, it should be due to a lack of resources (staffing) and be temporary until the team is up to speed.

③ The Significance Of Being Present

Executives often ask what they can do to instill a culture of operational excellence within their organizations. My response is straightforward: Just Show Up. In today's fast-paced digital age, where distractions are abundant, genuine presence is increasingly rare yet essential. Emails and memos stating you value continuous improvement and operational excellence are meaningless if your physical presence is absent from the initiatives. Demonstrating your active involvement has proven to be one of the most influential lessons I impart to executives.

One of the most powerful tools I leveraged was a simple, straightforward monthly meeting. I asked three to four teams monthly to present their completed projects to the management team. But more importantly, the company's president *always* sat front and center. The aim was not to create an atmosphere of intimidation; rather, it was for him to personally express gratitude to individuals for their ideas and contributions and underscore the significance of these projects to the company's financial success. Securing direct acknowledgment from the president, highlighting one's contribution, and motivating fellow employees to do the same provided unparalleled recognition. This meeting served as a platform to showcase employees' creativity. The profound effect of these interactions, where the president personally reviewed, acknowledged, and thanked associates, surpassed the impact of any email or generic statement displayed within the workplace.

Being physically present and attentive is one of the simplest yet most impactful ways to exhibit leadership and grow relationships. The mere act of showing up communicates a powerful message about what is prioritized. When projects hit roadblocks, the dynamic can drastically shift when a senior manager appears for an update.

The effectiveness of management is entirely undermined when they attend meetings while absorbed in their laptops or cell phones. Their divided attention signals that they are disengaged, which sends a message to those present that they are not significant enough to warrant the manager's focus. Our presence is communicated through our body language when interacting with others. Maintaining eye contact, displaying genuine interest, and posing meaningful questions demonstrate respect and appreciation for the time of others.

4 Validating Employees' Ideas Through Data Analysis

One of the biggest challenges in operational excellence is identifying and working with the best and brightest. One would think they would be easily identified and praised for their contributions. The opposite is true.

Some of the most valuable contributors to an organization are highly introverted individuals with diverse backgrounds and extensive experience. Their creativity in problem-solving is second to none, but they are known to question their own thoughts and ideas. Their ability to ask insightful questions enhances their understanding and inspires others to do the same. They understand how little they know and constantly seek to broaden their understanding. They may give a quick answer, pause, and reevaluate with more depth as information is presented to them. Unfortunately, their approach can be misconstrued as a lack of confidence in their solution, leading to their ideas being overlooked in favor of less thoughtful solutions during meetings.

Employees who are highly extroverted or outspoken can result in individuals confidently presenting information, even when they lack substantial knowledge or background in the subject matter. It's surprising how often individuals with lower levels of education or experience yet possess exceptional debate or presentation skills can disproportionately influence decision-making processes. Unfortunately, this behavior is sometimes unintentionally rewarded, resulting in investing time and money in ideas that may not be thoroughly examined. I've become keenly aware of their sensitivity to distorted or exaggerated information through hundreds of conversations with frustrated employees.

The loss of managerial respect is inevitable when employees perceive decision-making processes as popularity contests rather than relying on data-driven conversations to vet information and solutions. This erodes employee trust and morale and significantly threatens your operational excellence journey. Establishing an environment of transparency and evidence-based decision-making is crucial for minimizing unnecessary risk within the organization.

Prevent bias toward employees by demanding supportable and reproducible data to support all proposals or solutions. This approach levels the playing field for everyone. Regardless of an individual's ability to persuasively present their idea, having data to support it ensures everyone understands the basis of a recommendation.

Ensure everyone is educated on what kind of information is sought and encourage it to be presented in simple terms. It's common to have biased data and lack a complete understanding of the underlying assumptions. Data must be explained in a way a nontechnical person can comprehend. Excessive use of jargon and overwhelming data mask the lack of true understanding of an issue. Create a culture where issues and failures are openly discussed. Will the data be quickly dismissed if it doesn't present the narrative desired?

Demand everyone to bring data to every problem/solution discussion to ensure productive meetings instead of debates. Evaluate the quality of the teams' questions and observe how the data is interpreted. This approach highlights hidden talents, even if they are introverted or more analytical than argumentative. Give them the time and space needed to articulate their thoughts fully. A well-structured session will give a clearer understanding of the issues at hand, speed up the problem-solving process, and provide better direction for the next steps.

5 Developing An Effective Communication Strategy

One of the biggest mistakes I see repeated is the countless hours invested in creating a new product, new infrastructure, or policies just to have them fail during implementation. The fatal flaw isn't in the plan itself but rather in the insufficient communication of the impending changes. So much time is spent planning that communication plans are forgotten or not distributed well in advance to everyone who will be affected. Poor communication implies that change isn't important. Repetition is vital to ensure the message gets across and its importance is communicated to the organization.

The communication challenges become apparent when evaluating the inventory of technology and software applications. Although communication ideally should flow seamlessly throughout the organization like a river, it often scatters like rain, occasionally reaching the intended recipients while bypassing others. Agreement on specific communication methods becomes crucial. As teams expand, individuals tend to rely on communication channels that suit them, leading to fragmentation—from texts to instant messages to emails. Over time, people must piece together scattered data points like a jigsaw puzzle, causing unnecessary complexity and confusion.

Let's look at some typical communications and how they are often handled.

Strategic Objectives. Are all employees, from facilities to the C-suite, well-versed in the core organizational objectives? In most organizations, only the management team understands the message and need for urgency. Front-line employees are challenged to translate objectives into actionable tasks, leading to a lack of alignment. The most effective organizations cascade these objectives down through individual KPIs tied to performance reviews. This requires a streamlined process and supporting infrastructure, often assisted by software. Unfortunately, the responsibility of cascading the message typically rests with the management team, and the effectiveness of this dissemination can vary, resulting in missed opportunities for alignment across all levels of the organization.

Policy Changes. Policy changes are common, and very little thought is given to how the messages will be deployed. They tend to be mentioned during meetings or sent via email. But what happens if staff members miss a meeting, don't read the email, or misunderstand the change? How long before a missed communication or a miscommunication is realized? I've seen cases where people do things incorrectly for years because they "missed the memo," and no one took the time to go back and audit for compliance on the new changes. If the policy change is significant, investing time and effort to ensure the message is delivered and understood is also important. Spend time creating a strategy on:

- **Delivering Policy Changes:** Carefully plan how policy changes are communicated, ensuring effective dissemination across the organization.

- **Centralized Storage:** Establish a centralized repository for policies, eliminating the need for employees to create their individual filing systems ensuring easy access and consistency.

- **Regular Reviews:** Set a regular schedule for policy reviews, ensuring they are up-to-date and align with the organization's evolving needs and objectives.

Reorganizations. One of the greatest organizational challenges lies in effectively communicating changes in job assignments, promotions, or reporting structures. Managers are often unaware of all the people and processes impacted by the reorganization. Typically, changes are communicated through brief memos distributed to a limited audience.

When employees leave and the decision is made not to replace their position, their workload is often distributed among others in the organization. These subtle changes in job responsibilities are seldom communicated well across the organization. Over time, this creates a series of knowledge gaps of who is responsible for what tasks. Initially, this leads to confusion as employees attempt to understand their new roles and duties. Gaps in process handoffs are common during this transition, and if structure and clear guidance are not given, employees will interpret and implement policies and procedures in unintended ways.

Newly promoted or moved staff are also unlikely to have knowledge of all the reports and data available to them. Review the level of transparency of key KPIs and dashboards, the reports available, what information they contain, who receives them, and in what format (inbox, permission-protected team share areas, etc.). Clear communication and access to vital data are pivotal in ensuring informed decision-making and reducing organizational risk.

What is your process for handling reorganizations?

- Is there an established process to quickly update email/report distributions and organizational charts?

- Where are job descriptions maintained to provide clarity on roles and responsibilities within the organization?

- Promotions involve a transition of duties. How does the organization fully understand the change? How difficult is it for employees to relearn who's responsible for tasks and who their new contact is? A stronger process for transitioning staff would ensure a quicker learning curve, leading to a reduced productivity loss in the organization.

Emergency Communications. Speed is of the essence here. Most companies with a good emergency plan have automated messages to phones or, at the least, phone trees to get the message out. Does the company adhere to its own documented policies, or does it quickly go into firefighting mode?

There are multiple strategies to optimize communication.

- **Review All Communication Channels:** Conduct a full inventory and review of the content and methods employed for information dissemination across the organization. Where is important information stored? Develop a deep understanding and review of document repositories, the use of email (the black hole of information), chat and messaging systems, calendars, meetings, and meeting notes (or lack thereof). Is intellectual property properly secured and managed?

- **Utilize Discussion Boards:** Replace unnecessary meetings with discussion boards where information can be shared efficiently.

A well-organized discussion board can function as a team portal, accommodating various forms of communication, such as meeting notes and project updates.

• **Delegate Representatives:** Effective communication can often be achieved by assigning representatives from adjacent teams to attend each other's meetings. This ensures the smooth flow of information between teams and enhances collaboration.

• **Host Roundtable Discussions:** Organize monthly or quarterly roundtable discussions to address issues or concerns that may not be suitable for regular meetings. These sessions provide a platform to raise specific challenges and allow teams to collaborate, enabling the identification of problematic areas in other teams' processes.

(6) Utilizing Training For Operational Excellence

A commonly overlooked area for strategy and infrastructure lies within training programs. Continuous learning is imperative in today's ever-changing business landscape. Training consumes substantial resources and serves various purposes, including onboarding new hires, instructing job roles, or educating external customers. However, in today's fast-paced world of short attention spans, marked by platforms like X (formerly Twitter), there is a significant reluctance to invest time in reading, learning, and practicing new techniques despite the potential benefits. Yet, employee or product training is expected to be the exception. A good training program equips employees with the ability to adapt and meet the challenges of today's ever-changing landscape.

Onboarding And Job Training

An often-overlooked aspect that significantly impacts operational excellence is the onboarding and training process for new hires. Sadly, few organizations invest adequate resources to ensure uniformity and quality across the entire organization. While organizations might provide structured training at the corporate level, departmental training often lacks consistency, varying widely in execution from onboarding to job training, with content scattered across multiple formats and locations.

Many teams lack in-depth knowledge about the skill sets present within their group or adjacent teams. Recognizing that the skills needed today might not align with those needed tomorrow, implementing and upkeeping a skills matrix provides a clear view of the expertise within teams and their proficiency levels. By comprehending both the proficiencies and possible skill gaps within a team, proactive cross-training initiatives can be put in place. Implementing a skills matrix serves as a safeguard against employees with limited skill mastery training others or conveying incorrect knowledge or techniques. By conducting proficiency assessments, the risk of poor techniques or non-compliance with standards causing an increase in defects or high-profile failures can be mitigated effectively.

Conduct a high-level strategic review of training content and flow to ensure all team members receive and comprehend the necessary information. Lacking a standardized training approach can introduce variations that might lead to future defects and inefficiencies within the organization. Consider the following:

- How do new team members achieve mastery?
- How is their proficiency in the training program validated?
- Who conducts the training and onboarding sessions?
- Does the trainer possess the necessary skills to ensure accurate transmission of cultural and informational aspects?

Using software to compensate for a lack of a skill set or reduce the need for a higher skill set—automation—can quickly backfire. Automation, when overused, can create complexities and additional costs in the long run. A more sustainable approach involves identifying knowledge gaps within the team and providing resources and incentives for skill development. Cultivating a continuous learning culture empowers employees to contribute their best ideas without burdening the organization with legacy processes or intricate software challenges.

Leverage the expertise of experienced team members by implementing mentorship programs. Pair less experienced employees with seasoned mentors who can guide them in honing their skills. Additionally, reverse mentoring, where younger staff mentor senior employees in newer technologies, can bridge generational skill gaps effectively.

Training To Mask Process Failures

When the need for extensive training arises to grasp a new process or acquaint customers with fresh product features, it raises a crucial question: "Why is it so complicated?" Training to address complexity is often a red flag, indicating underlying issues in the system's design or processes.

As new technologies age and become legacy systems, workarounds are introduced, creating convoluted processes that evolve over time—with various people *adding* steps rather than reengineering processes to meet the stated requirements. Workarounds tackle the symptoms of the problem and leave the problem intact. Think of software with so many "add-ons" that it becomes almost unusable as users try remembering weird keystroke combinations to complete a task.

Frequently, organizations resort to temporary solutions like extensive training or checklists when delving into root causes seems daunting due to time or energy constraints. However, these solutions come with their own challenges.

1. **Impact On Staff Focus And Productivity:** Introducing new training or processes demands a shift in staff focus. Employees must invest time learning and mastering these new techniques or processes, diverting their attention from existing tasks. This reallocation of time can impact productivity in current, pressing responsibilities.

2. **Challenges In Ensuring Compliance:** Mere demonstration of a new process doesn't guarantee full compliance. It also requires significant time dedicated to auditing the process, ensuring the correct implementation of the new technique. Regular checks and evaluations ensure the new technique is learned and correctly integrated into daily practices. Continuous monitoring guarantees sustained adherence to the established standards.

3. **Difficulty In Learning:** Lengthy training sessions or extensive written instructions often result in challenges for learners, hindering the effective execution of tasks. Consider the common scenario of assembling furniture from IKEA: faced with a lengthy instruction manual, individuals may feel overwhelmed and tempted to skip steps or delay the process.

4. **Failures In Real-Life Scenarios:** In an extreme example, it was discovered that in an air emergency, some checklists, if followed, would take up to thirty minutes to complete. While pilots are trained to follow protocol, a 30-minute checklist is impossible if the plane suffers an emergency and every second is critical.

5. **Diminishing Training Efficacy:** Training for infrequently performed tasks is ineffective as individuals tend to forget instructions over time. In such instances, relying on checklists proves invaluable, provided they are regularly reviewed and revised.

When training is necessary, invest in comprehensive, targeted sessions. Provide clear explanations, practical demonstrations, and interactive learning experiences to facilitate effective knowledge transfer. Continuously review and update checklists, aligning them with the latest best practices and insights. Supplement textual instructions with visual aids or, better yet, video instruction. Simple work sequences and instructions that can be quickly understood and remembered take more time to develop. The benefits outweigh the time spent creating them.

Better yet, encourage a full redesign to minimize the need for training in the first place. Take the suggestion for additional product or process training instead of a full review of what started the conversation in the first place:

1. Identify Complicated Processes

2. Review Excessive Add-on Steps Or Features

3. Embrace User-Centric Design

4. Prioritize Simplicity

5. Promote Clear Instructions

(7) Data-Driven Decision Making

Data collection aims to make informed decisions, not simply to report. Data serves as the objective language used when discussing issues. Technology facilitates the gathering and use of data. It increases visibility and highlights areas of concern. It helps us understand the magnitude of the problem and guide us through changes. Data helps us establish baseline performance levels and know when a process needs to be recalibrated to the standard.

There is a caveat to data; it's valuable only if it brings meaningful business insights. Excessively collected metrics can turn overwhelming, drowning in irrelevant noise that fails to enhance decision-making. The key lies in presenting information in a manner that others can comprehend, allowing them to understand its origins and validate its accuracy.

One of the most misused metrics involves using averages in performance metrics: average service levels, average call volume in call centers, or average sales per representative. While averages provide a broad overview of process performance, the outliers contain the real story to be understood. Managing outliers dramatically affects the averages. Consider this example: if two people take a test and one person scores 100 percent and the other scores 0 percent, the average is 50 percent. Looking solely at this average might suggest the entire program needs to be revamped since *everyone* failed. But upon closer inspection, it becomes clear only one person needs attention. The average would have ensured everyone passed if this person had scored higher. Averages punish high performers while hiding the issues of underperformers. Ask a top-performing salesperson how they feel about policies aimed at the lowest performer versus policies that reward top performers.

One of the most misused metrics involves using averages in performance metrics: average service levels, average call volume in call centers, or average sales per representative. While averages provide a broad overview of process performance, the outliers contain the real story to be understood.

As working with data becomes easier, introduce complexity by integrating internal data with external sources—such as purchased data sets or publicly available information like census data. Use software that facilitates fast data extraction for continual monitoring. It's common to discover data isn't being accurately tracked, uncovering gaps previously overlooked. Ensuring accurate data tracking by focusing on the right information is a key component of implementing new solutions.

Becoming comfortable with simple but powerful analytics will bring more insightful questions and a deeper understanding. Consider focusing on the following key areas:

- Sales Force Performance
  - Number of sales and returns by salesperson
- Customer Loyalty And Profitability
  - Number of purchases, frequency of purchases, and referrals
- Customer Satisfaction
  - Number of returns and support calls
- Product Quality
  - Cancellations, returns, and calls to tech support
- Process Metrics
  - Accuracy, efficiency, and defect rate
  - Lead versus process time
  - Complexity and cost of workarounds
- Integrated Employee View
  - Performance metrics
  - Training assessment
  - Skill mastery/deficiency evaluations
  - Employee engagement levels

Technology has ushered in a new wave of new capabilities in data analysis, enabling us to:

- Train Predictive Algorithms
- Sense The Physical World In Real-Time
  - Utilize ocular and environmental sensors
- Augment Reality

- Enhance Our Security Posture
- Gain A 360-Degree Customer View:
  - Analyze transactional history and behavioral patterns
  - Incorporate the voice of the customer through call recordings and speech analytics
  - Collect comprehensive information to build a robust customer profile.

Beware of the deficiencies in data collection:

- Data Silos: Information is fragmented across numerous software platforms, leading to redundancy and inefficiency.

- Data Quality Neglect: Emphasis on data quality is lacking, resulting in unstructured data formats (emails, PowerPoint, chats) that are challenging to analyze and act upon.

- Access Management Issues: Permissions are not developed strategically, causing employees to have either excessive or insufficient data access. Employees are often unaware of the data collected and storage locations.

- Absence Of Formal Policies: There are no established data policies covering governance, storage location, proper collection methods, auditing, data retention, etc.

- Storage Challenges: Data stored in various platforms and formats creates high storage costs, poses security risks, and lacks visibility.

Finally, only measure where it drives business impact, avoiding data collection just for the sake of it. The amount of time wasted on collecting and preparing seldom-used data is astonishing. In some cases, data collected is reviewed so late it is outdated and serves only as a retrospective view of past events instead of timely information. As much as possible, prioritize leading indicators in processes to enhance real-time risk management and decision-making.

CHAPTER 5

The Teams

8 Balancing Authority And Responsibility In Decision-Making

While empowering teams to make decisions is crucial, there are instances where they exceed their decision-making authority unintentionally and without harmful intentions. Development and engineering teams, in particular, tend to modify features or processes beyond agreed specifications and without full team approval. Common justifications include:

- **Perceiving it as a minor alteration:** Changes are viewed as insignificant and assumed they wouldn't impact the outcome.

- **Urgent decision-making:** In cases of urgency, decisions are made without adequate time for consultation or notification of the original team.

- **Necessity due to unfeasible process design:** The original design was deemed unfeasible for a reason, and an alternative was implemented without consulting the team for impact.

There are a few ways the situation unfolds. Sometimes, it begins with teams who don't have a good way to check for agreement *and* commitment. How many meetings end where people assume tasks will be completed but were never fully committed to? Would you tell someone, "We should go out sometime," and expect them to be at your favorite restaurant at 5:00 p.m. on Friday? It seems silly to even imagine, but how many times do we hear people in meetings say things like, "it might be possible," "I suppose," or "maybe after the next project," and then assume they have agreed to the idea or are supporting its completion? Drill down and get team members to agree to specific timelines and work so obstacles or existing objections are understood. When writing down all the main steps of a project, potential bottlenecks will likely surface that, if unresolved, will delay or kill a project.

Human nature tends to foster hope and optimism, often leading us to believe that things might miraculously work out. It might, of course, but why waste time and energy on something that won't happen or put time and energy into removing obstacles to ensure success? Checking for agreement will increase understanding of the realistic possibilities of success and reduce the risk of being blindsided by the unexpected.

Another reason is teams have been allowed to make changes with no repercussions. The behavior continues unchecked until an event causes a full analysis of how a defect or issue was created and points back to a decision that was not authorized.

Sometimes, a decision is made in the midst of firefighting, but the team doesn't think to revisit the decision with the entire team at the earliest opportunity. Many of these changes may go unnoticed or simply ignored because they did not cause immediate problems. It creates a subtle signal to the team members that this behavior is sanctioned as part of the process. In other words, the message delivered is that changes required to meet a deadline are authorized without full consent or even awareness by the broader team.

First, let's acknowledge these scenarios are common, and review all processes to ensure transparency instead of secrecy. There are a few ways the team can ensure awareness. If the teams conduct regular stand-up meetings, it's important to specifically call out any changes to the original plan, whether or not issues have been created to date because of them. This is a critical distinction; many members would not think to mention a change if they didn't believe the change caused any harm. If there are no regular stand-up meetings, then a change management process alerts teams of changes made between regular check-ins that could potentially affect other dependences they are unaware of.

In an ideal world, teams would be calibrated to understand when deviations from original plans require additional authorization or, minimally, a notification of a decision that had to be made quickly so the entire team has time to reflect upon any future impact.

9 Building Psychological Safety

"If management only knew."

"It will never work!"

How often are you surprised by situations that appear to escalate with little warning? Statements like the ones above need to be addressed quickly. It's a sign of today's modern times how technology and a culture of careful conversations have led to an epidemic of dysfunctional communication. In a world of texting, chat, and remote work, our communication has become so efficient it's ineffective.

I had the opportunity to hear Travis Hahler, Google's neuroscientist, speak. He used a powerful example of how good intentions can quickly backfire to demonstrate the challenges of change management from a neuroscientist's perspective. When a friend tells us their dog died, we instinctively know there is grief and the importance of listening and comforting. We would never be callous in looking at the positive side of the dog's death, such as money saved in veterinary bills or increased personal time by not needing to care for the dog. When discussing change in the workplace, such as a new role, a reorganization, or a new supervisor, we immediately try to find all the positive things involved in the change. We don't stop to consider the loss and grief experienced in the loss of routine, being forced to learn a new skill, or having new coworkers. We automatically assume change will be good for everyone.

Google spent years attempting to find the secret sauce to highly successful teams through a project they named Aristotle. According to Google's research, the most important element of successful teams—and I would argue for a successful company—is the amount of psychological safety that exists.[8]

Psychological safety is key to success in continuous improvement. It refers to a shared belief that it is safe to take interpersonal risks, such as sharing ideas, asking questions, or expressing concerns without fear of negative consequences. Language plays a defining role in creating psychological safety and building a culture of operational excellence. Disclosing a potential problem should be rewarded, not punished. How often have situations been created where we inadvertently trained employees to lie or hide information from us? In the journey to transform culture, look hard at the words and phrases most heard around the company. What meaning do they imply? Do they encourage positive behavior, or do they demean and derail employees?

The presence of toxic individuals can profoundly erode the psychological safety within a team, giving rise to an unhealthy and stressful workplace atmosphere. Such individuals often exhibit judgmental behavior, criticism, or even engage in bullying. Consequently, diverse perspectives within the team may be suppressed, curbing the contributions and initiatives of others.

Toxic behaviors can foster the creation of silos among team members, impeding collaboration and mutual support. This isolation limits the free flow of ideas and cooperation, hindering the team's overall effectiveness. Dealing with a toxic team member can exact an emotional toll on individuals, negatively impacting their psychological well-being over time.

If left unaddressed, the toxic dynamic can lead to a deterioration of trust and respect among team members. This breakdown in foundational elements further exacerbates the challenges of maintaining a psychologically safe environment, ultimately undermining the team's ability to thrive and collaborate effectively.

Being mindful of the unintentional messages sent will allow you to consciously model new behavior and carefully select the vocabulary to send a clear, positive message of what is valued. Pay attention to the stories shared throughout the company; what tone is used, and what warnings are shared among employees? Stories shared can inspire and engage employees while providing valuable lessons about culture and values.

10 The Importance Of A Shared Vocabulary

A powerful way to underscore the importance of a shared language is to show a team the picture above. I ask the team to take a look, process the image, and then ask, "Is this a good piece of art?" I start by giving them no context, so they are left to evaluate good through their own bias and perspective. I then pose a series of questions:

- What if I told you a five-year-old did the painting? Do you think it's good?

- What if I told you the painting was a Banksy? Do you think it's good?

- What if I told you a novice adult painter did the painting? Do you still think it's good?

I then give them the real answer. The painting was created by an elephant and done as a self-portrait. Hearing the artist is an animal, most people will agree that the painting is *good*.

Let's begin by trying to unravel the subjectivity of "good." Consider the complexity of aligning perspectives within a team about what constitutes "good" work processes, standards, and performance. Words like "quality," "good," and "better," which are integral to team objectives, often result in diverse interpretations among team members. A lack of shared understanding of common words and phrases used by the team are sources of confusion and misunderstanding and the root cause of process breakdowns. It's common for several members to reject work others might readily approve.

Consider a common scenario: a team member requests business requirements for building a report. They asked for a *list of key uses* for the information so the builder could derive what data points were required to fulfill the needs of the person requesting it. Instead, the person received a *list of data points* without a rationale for using the data. What's the difference? The first person used the traditional definition of a business requirement: critical activities needed to be performed to meet the organizational objective(s) while remaining *solution independent*. The second person defined a business requirement as the *solutions themselves*. This led to several confusing conversations and interactions where two people used the same term but had two different definitions.

This divergence in understanding creates a profound challenge: inconsistent quality and standards become pervasive, affecting every team member. When context is lacking, individuals tend to fill the gaps with their assumptions or biases, creating a spectrum of interpretations. How can we expect harmonious collaboration and cohesive efforts when the very benchmarks we strive for lack a unified definition? Addressing this fundamental discrepancy is the key to fostering a shared vision of excellence within the team. Through clear communication and mutual agreement on these critical terms, we pave the way for a collective pursuit of quality and performance that truly aligns with our objectives.

Every team speaks its own remixed language of technical jargon and office acronyms. As a facilitator, I am an archeologist deciphering a hieroglyphic while trying to win office bingo. Dysfunctionality often doesn't lie within the team itself but in the realm of communication. My lack of subject matter expertise while I facilitated is what made me effective. I ask the questions no one would think to ask because everyone assumes they are having the same conversation.

To mitigate these challenges, begin by checking to see how much agreement there is on common terms and objectives. Areas for team improvement are likely to be uncovered. Make it part of the team process to stop and check for agreement on important terms in their functional area. In a software team, does everyone agree on what's included in a "sandbox" versus "production" environment? In a call center, does everyone understand the definition of a "good call?" By checking for agreement, a foundation is created for a highly aligned team that is not slowed down by constant miscommunication. The reverse is a team that allows simple issues to escalate to a point where a supervisor has to get involved to help solve team dysfunction (lack of performance, personnel issues, etc.).

When everyone understands common department- and company-wide terminology, conversations become fluid with less likelihood of misinterpretation. Continue by spending time establishing a process to create and review standardized definitions periodically. This shared understanding serves as a foundational framework, enabling the team to calibrate and refine their criteria for acceptable and unacceptable quality.

(11) Creating Focus And Managing Distractions

American workers are interrupted every eleven minutes and then spend almost a third of their day recovering from these distractions.[9] Despite believing multitasking compensates for lost time, only 2.5 percent of the population can effectively multitask.[10] Multitasking is continuous task switching, splitting our attention, and paying for it in time and effectiveness. Multitasking also introduces significant risk by creating opportunities for more mistakes. The more time spent switched to another task, the less likely you will return to the original task. The inevitable happens with additional stress as loose ends pile up.

The brain must process forty bits of information each second to understand what another person is saying. Assume the upper limit of our capacity to be sixty bits per second (based on current research)[11] to understand what three people are saying simultaneously is theoretically possible. However, this can only be done by managing to keep every other thought or sensation out of consciousness, including expressions and physical environments, to maintain focus.

In today's business environment, tools can quickly turn into distractions. Like all tools, email management tools, to-do lists, and phone apps need a strategy to be productive. It seems obvious that physical devices are useless without the skill to use them and a procedure for how they will be used. It's not as obvious; time also needs a strategy for spending it and which tools will be required.

In today's business environment, tools can quickly turn into distractions. Like all tools, email management tools, to-do lists, and phone apps need a strategy to be productive.

Strategic time management is an important component of team productivity. Teams need to internalize the value of their time and hold themselves accountable. Implementing and respecting time blocks designed to meet objectives. Employees' greatest asset is not their availability but their ability to solve problems and get things done. Being busy is not the same as being productive. Managers play a pivotal role in modeling the right behaviors, emphasizing fewer meetings, and fostering enhanced transparency in processes. Phone calls, emails, chats, meetings, and Zoom calls eat up hours of people's daily and weekly time and are rarely managed. Busy work, often used as a coping mechanism for mental or physical fatigue, is a pitfall that must be circumvented. Build in breaks in the form of less complex work on occasion as well as physical breaks to reduce the temptation of teams to succumb to distractions.

─────────────────────▽─────────────────────

Employees' greatest asset is not their availability but their ability to solve problems and get things done.

─────────────────────△─────────────────────

The Pareto principle teaches us that time should not be evenly distributed across all tasks. Employees need to understand where their presence and time can make the most significant impact. Take time to plan and understand what needs to be accomplished daily, weekly, and monthly. Prioritization is the cornerstone of efficient time management, enabling teams to focus on high-priority and high-impact tasks. Leverage tools and delegate items that may be necessary but produce little value.

When problem-solving, the temptation to tackle several issues can quickly overwhelm a team and its resources. Failure to drop one focus and move on to others creates loops of anxiety. The inability to disengage attention from one issue to focus on the next can turn productive reflection into analysis paralysis. One technique to keep a team moving forward is to put a tentative solution in place to prevent employees from obsessing over endless details. It is important to instill the idea of flexibility. Tentative solutions are subject to change when better data or more refined solutions become available.

Support the team's objectives by understanding how organizational time affects their work. Become mindful of where attention is given and make conscious decisions about where focus should be.

(12) A Tale Of Two Companies Adapting To Remote Work

The swift arrival of work-from-home mandates during the early stages of the COVID-19 pandemic provided an opportunity to observe how two companies navigated this challenge. The uniqueness of the situation stemmed from the stark contrast in their prior work structures. One company, accustomed to operating across seven different facilities, had experience with remote teams. In contrast, the other company primarily functioned within the confines of a physical office, with 98 percent of its work traditionally conducted on-site.

Let's start with the greater challenge: turning an office-only team into a work-from-home team. Thanks to a robust, continuous improvement culture, the shift was embraced with remarkable agility. Every team and employee started thinking about how to transition into remote work quickly. Teams began to think about skill sets and functions rather than roles and responsibilities. Call centers posed unique challenges because they were designed to be in person. To confront this challenge, our technical support department created ad hoc teams to support and assist the information technology (IT) department through the transition. Leveraging their technical skills allowed them to share the internal support workload. To lessen unnecessary movement, staff quickly determined who lived close to each other and arranged to have equipment delivered to those who needed it. New technologies were quickly learned, new guidelines were set, and existing processes were reviewed for their adaptability for remote support.

In both organizations, employees took charge, offering insights and recommendations to the management teams regarding processes and infrastructure. This proactive approach stood out significantly. Instead of waiting for decisions to trickle down, employees actively engaged in shaping the transition. Management remained in the loop, having the chance to make necessary corrections as informed changes were implemented. Comparatively, other companies experienced slower transitions. Remarkably, within a mere two weeks, our company achieved a remarkable 95 percent remote capability.

The second company was primarily comprised of engineers and personnel in light manufacturing. Since the developers and engineers were global teams accustomed to remote work, the major challenges came from transitioning physical environments into home environments. Engineers who worked with physical equipment or field teams had to find ways to do testing and development work differently. Supply chains were disrupted, there were unexpected bottlenecks, and quick product redesigns were required to minimize the impact.

From observing both teams, here are some things I discovered:

• **Employee Problem-Solving**: When given an opportunity to problem solve, most employees embrace the challenge.

• **Decentralized Decision-Making**: Relying on management, especially when they lack comprehensive data, can lead to problems. Empowering individuals closest to the work to devise initial solutions and guiding them with managerial insights is a more effective approach.

• **Maintaining Team Connection**: Teams and employees who had worked and spent time together faced challenges preserving their connections when suddenly separated. Relationships require effort. While technology allows for constant communication, the absence of physical proximity can weaken bonds over time. Building a supportive infrastructure is crucial to sustain remote team relationships.

• **Informal Idea Exchange**: Some of the best ideas happen informally during moments like a shower or a walk. These insights are casually shared in break rooms or during lunch in office settings. Fostering an environment that encourages the free exchange of random thoughts becomes essential when working remotely. Creating avenues for informal communication is vital for nurturing creativity and innovation among remote teams.

(13) Maximizing Creativity By Harnessing And Implementing Ideas

I have discovered there are two main approaches to idea generation. The first is to stay abreast of the latest business trends and market innovations. The second is to find ways to expose employees to new ideas in an organic way and help them generate their own.

Develop good sources for information. I quickly found the value in subscribing to curated news subscriptions such as Smartbrief or book summary services such as Summary.com. Finding good sources of curated information is critical to getting concise and comprehensive information to keep a pulse on today's business climate. Hubspot has a great newsletter called The Hustle, and websites like Interesting Engineering cover innovation from many perspectives in a large variety of industries. I found this particularly useful as many interesting solutions I encountered were in industries very far removed from my own.

Capture good ideas in meetings. Organizations overlook the importance of creating a structured ideation process, leading to lost ideas and redundant efforts. Despite generating ideas in meetings, these ideas often vanish into forgotten meeting notes or obscure files. An effective process for idea capture includes a standardized form to record pertinent details and a systematic notification system to engage relevant stakeholders. Proper documentation and action-taking mechanisms are crucial in transforming raw ideas into actionable outcomes. Meetings, including virtual ones, should be recorded and transcribed, ensuring no valuable insights are lost in the conversation flow.

I have discovered there are two main approaches to idea generation. The first is to stay abreast of the latest business trends and market innovations. The second is to find ways to expose employees to new ideas in an organic way and help them generate their own.

Use unfamiliarity. With process workflows, one way to get a fresh perspective and new ideas is to find someone unfamiliar with the process and ask them to complete a task, such as completing a transaction. This exercise highlights redundant steps, complexity, and inefficiencies, guiding teams to simplify processes organically before considering technological interventions that only serve to link disjointed process flows.

Review customer data. Reviewing data collected from a customer can often show that redundant information is being requested that can be obtained from internal systems. If this is the case, you can highlight this as an indicator that dataflows need to be reviewed and optimized.

Free teams from functional fixedness. Another way to spark new ideas involves changing your team's mindset. Many people can be held back in creating new ideas by functional fixedness which is a term describing an individual's inability to see an object's potential uses beyond its intended purpose. This cognitive limitation hampers creativity, hindering the ability to think outside the box quite literally. Why does this matter? Over time, teams grow accustomed to conventional uses of items, forgetting that almost everything possesses multifaceted utility. For instance, adults might perceive a cardboard box solely as a shipping container, while a child transforms it into countless imaginative objects through play. Recognizing and overcoming this fixed mindset is essential for fostering innovation within teams.

Send your teams out. Encourage teams to attend and participate in industry meetings and conferences to broaden their perspectives. It is imperative to encourage active engagement, including note-taking and photo documentation, with a knowledge-sharing mandate.

Discourage associates from simply viewing these opportunities as a way to spend a day away from the office.

Education is key: empower employees to leverage every idea-generation opportunity. Collaborative projects enable employees to exchange insights, best practices, and innovative ideas. Organizations can significantly enhance their problem-solving capabilities and eliminate redundant efforts by centralizing ideas and using this repository as a knowledge hub. Minimize bureaucratic hurdles and administrative complexities in the ideation process to avoid discouraging future initiatives. The inability to initiate or execute ideas can significantly hinder the success of any program. Stories of frustrated employees with unacknowledged ideas will quickly spread through the organization and harm the culture you are trying to create.

CHAPTER 6

The Tools

(14) Capturing Reality Beyond Conventional Process Mapping

Since starting my CI journey, one of the biggest changes of the past decade is the landscape of work observations. Thanks to technology, we now have the ability to conduct observations from various perspectives. It's crucial to exploit these technological advancements fully, eliminating the reliance on flawed recollections and outdated process diagrams that often fail to capture the true essence of work dynamics.

While teams frequently discuss workplace challenges, the importance of physically witnessing the operations often gets overlooked. Challenge teams to go where the work is done and understand firsthand the nuances of the process. Process mapping is usually done from memory, with little verification that the steps and time estimates are accurate: it becomes a memory game on which future decisions will be based.

Mistakes can be a key to finding real improvements. Things happening before our eyes are missed, and memories are incredibly fallible when physically observing. I remember the time I pulled out a cell phone on a manufacturing floor to record a process we were trying to improve. This was a critical difference from the normal method of mapping out a process in a conference room away from where the real work is done, working from memory to recreate the steps in the process and often guessing how long each step took instead of getting an accurate time.

I wanted to record a simple packing process. The observations were eye-opening. We had spent significant money on building workstations with proper tables. However, the team members opted for a makeshift approach of placing a cardboard piece on top of a trash can. Their reasoning was clear—they wanted more flexibility in their work while avoiding moving back and forth within the manufacturing cell. However, this preference resulted in frequent mishaps; essential tools like tape and scissors often found their way to the floor, requiring time for retrieval and reorganization.

The "steps" of dropping tools and utilizing makeshift tables are usually absent in conventional process maps. This discrepancy highlights a common issue: distractions and mistakes are usually not captured in process mapping and are dismissed as isolated incidents. It's no wonder that process-improvement solutions fail at the point of implementation. Work in a real environment is full of distractions, defective raw materials, tired associates, or lack of resources.

Technology offers diverse methods to precisely document processes:

- **Cell phone recording**: Simply grab a cell phone and record, enabling the review of interactions between individuals and equipment. Such recordings facilitate accurate time tracking for each process step. While our eyes perceive numerous activities, our brains selectively store information. One can uncover the reality of operations by recording processes and revisiting them later, individually or as a group. What distractions or errors characterize the existing process? What hampers establishing a streamlined process, free from rework and interruptions? Analyzing recorded footage provides valuable insights into these critical questions.

- **Screen recording**: Encourage teams to utilize screen recording tools in an office setting. Numerous free or low-cost software solutions will allow teams to capture their computer screen activities. This will allow you to view the constant handoffs between software applications, review double-entry tasks, and pinpoint potential human errors. Several phone systems have this feature integrated into their phone systems as well.

- **Phone recording**: Implement phone call recording to gain valuable insights into agent performance and identify training opportunities. Recording phone interactions accurately depicts a customer's tone and experience during the call. Utilizing speech analytics, if enabled, allows for sentiment analysis and keyword recognition. For a comprehensive view of customer and agent experiences, consider integrating phone and screen recording. This integrated approach offers a holistic perspective that can significantly enhance customer service strategies.

Relying solely on sticky notes on a wall is no longer adequate for achieving a profound understanding of a process. Consider implementing a high-level process mapping exercise that incorporates collecting and sharing samples for each step. These samples could include marketing collateral, emails, templates, screen recordings of the process, recorded customer calls, and more. Having the team collectively review these artifacts can achieve a more comprehensive and nuanced understanding of the discussed process.

Utilize the recordings for a detailed examination of each step and to capture the time taken in the process accurately. It's crucial to ensure that the right individuals are present in the room during these discussions, allowing for a thorough examination and facilitating the answering of questions related to the process at hand. This approach enhances the overall depth and clarity of the team's comprehension regarding the intricacies of the process under consideration.

15 The Tools: Using A SIPOC To Problem-Solve Effectively

Process Owner: Pizza Baker Process: Making Pepperoni Pizza			SIPOC	Boundaries: Includes/Excludes: Pizza Process, No Appliances	
Suppliers 3	**Inputs** 1		**Process** 5	**Outputs** 2	**Customers** 4
(Providers Of The Inputs)	(Resources Required)	Quality Issues (x)	Top Level Press Steps (5-7 steps only)	(Deliverables)	(Output Recipient)
			Requirements		
Restaurant Supply	Water		up to 450 degrees 1 Pre-Heat Oven	Pizza	Pizza Eater
Water Company	Dough (Water, Oil,	X		Breadsticks	
	Flour, Yeast, Etc.)		2 Prepare Dough		
Electric Company	Pepperoni			Calzones	
Farmer's Market	Cheese			Trash	
Grocery Store	Pizza Cutter		3 Spread Sauce		
	Pizza Sauce				
	Oven		4 Add Toppings		
	Pizza Stone				
	Table				
	Rolling Pin		5 Cook In Oven		
	Electricity				
	Mixing Bowls		6 Cut And Serve		
	Pizza Boxes				
Supplier Issues	**Input Metrics (Quality)**		**Process Metrics Breakdown/Adjust**	**Output Metrics (Performance)**	**Customer Pain Points**
Ingredient Quality Changed	Ingredient Quality			Pizza Taste (Rating)	

One of the most effective tools for identifying key problem drivers is the SIPOC (suppliers, inputs, process, outputs, customers) template. A SIPOC is conducted with all the stakeholders present— anyone with knowledge of the process or any of the inputs. When utilized collaboratively, a SIPOC can quickly identify issues and reveal the stakeholders and areas impacted, setting the stage for targeted improvement initiatives. Several textbooks will advise you to keep things at a high level. I find this is a mistake. In my experience, the details will likely bring the issues needed for improvement. Data collected during this process will drive changes as needed.

Let's analyze the SIPOC framework.

INPUTS - A Deep Dive Into Quality

In the SIPOC framework, the pivotal component is the inputs. This involves scrutinizing every element within the process. A comprehensive list of inputs is imperative to getting a broad view of an issue. Quality issues in the inputs will translate to poor process output or performance. While many textbooks advocate maintaining a high-level perspective, I argue against this approach. Frequently, the root of the problem lies in an overlooked input. If the solution were that obvious, the problem would have been resolved already.

Consider the example of making a pizza: this encompasses all ingredients, electricity, water, utensils, and work surfaces. The template is complete if the entire process can be replicated using the listed inputs. To emphasize the importance, I often ask, "If I provided you with all the inputs you listed and placed you in a parking lot, could you bake a pizza?" This usually highlights the need for the process to have a workspace, electricity, and appliances to complete the task, not just the ingredients.

As each input is examined, ask, "Are there any concerns or issues?" Think of the Pareto principle: one ingredient or issue, such as an oven that doesn't heat to the right temperature, is enough to ruin an entire pizza. Further examining our pizza process, I often ask teams if they know what gives New York-style pizza its distinctive taste. The answer is the water. Specifically, the water used in the dough. The mineral content in New York City's tap water is believed to result in a softer, more elastic dough. While other elements, like the type of flour and dough-making technique, also contribute to a good New York-style pizza, it's evident that adopting a high-level approach in the evaluation process wouldn't provide the necessary insight to address issues with the pizza's taste.

Garbage in, garbage out: it's as simple as that.

OUTPUTS - Evaluating Process Performance Through Outputs Analysis

Outputs directly reflect the process's performance, serving as vital indicators of its efficiency. Consider that the majority of an organization's Key Performance Indicators (KPIs) are intricately tied to these outputs. When evaluating outputs, the pivotal question arises: Is the end result meeting the anticipated standards—akin to assessing if the pizza tastes good—or is there a shortfall?

Output metrics often function as lagging indicators. When performance fails to align with expectations, pinpointing the exact area for improvement becomes daunting without pertinent quality metrics or leading indicators. Hence, maintaining a detailed inventory of all inputs and their related concerns becomes indispensable. This comprehensive approach provides the necessary groundwork for effective analysis and targeted enhancements in process efficiency.

Understanding how inputs influence the outputs is imperative. A single input can yield multiple outputs, just as multiple inputs can collectively contribute to a single output. Drawing parallels with the pizza analogy, all ingredients (multiple inputs) are imperative to yield one output (a pizza).

SUPPLIERS - Nurturing Quality Through Supplier Insight

The subsequent phase involves identifying all the suppliers responsible for the inputs. This knowledge is vital because understanding the supplier's identity is crucial if quality issues or concerns emerge related to an input. This information enables effective communication, allowing teams to gather additional insights and data about the situation. Often, a supplier undergoes a transition without the organization knowing, impacting the quality of the input. These transitions could be new employees and institutional knowledge lost, new management, a business rule change, or anything else that could impact a formerly stable process.

In the SIPOC framework, suppliers and customers are identified within the process, providing a comprehensive overview of all stakeholders involved.

OUTPUT - The Process Performance Metric

Outputs represent the outcomes of inputs. As previously emphasized, a significant portion of metrics focuses on outputs. Is the process in sync with the necessary speed, accuracy, and volume standards? In other words, does the performance of the outputs align effectively with the process requirements? Typically, a majority of your Key Performance Indicators (KPIs) and metrics are categorized as output metrics. However, when challenges arise, output metrics often fall short in providing insights into the underlying reasons for process or performance issues. This underscores the importance of balancing your output metrics with input metrics.

CUSTOMER - The Recipient Of The Output

The recipients of the process's outputs are its customers. An output might have multiple recipients. In the context of the pizza example, the customer for the pizza is the individual consuming it. It's crucial to note that customers aren't always individuals; they can also be entities like reports or software systems that receive inputs, such as data. Identifying these customers holds significance because if any issues arise with the output, the customer is the one who ensures that problems are rectified.

PROCESS

Finally, there is a five- to seven-step high-level overview of the process. This is not a process map but a high-level overview of the full process. This part of the diagram aims to identify any part of the process requiring a deeper dive and potentially one or multiple process diagrams.

For most issues, a SIPOC diagram can be completed within thirty to sixty minutes, assuming all the correct stakeholders are present. The value of the SIPOC will be in showing at a glance all of the elements, dependencies, people, and issues potentially driving suboptimal process performance.

16 Problem-Solving Foundations A Team Should Master

One of the difficulties in teaching problem-solving techniques is the tendency to want to teach associates the latest business trends and expect them to execute them well. The reality is that problem-solving methods are messy and unique to the individual, and epiphanies happen at random times with random triggers. By exposing people to different perspectives on the issues and how people in different industries have solved them, the possibility for innovation and creativity is greater. It's important associates solve problems their own way while increasing the tools in their toolbox (skill sets, methods, going to the place where work is done, etc.).

Make it OK to fail but encourage failing fast at the lowest cost possible with the highest amount of learning. Information and knowledge sharing must be encouraged to flow effortlessly throughout the organization to avoid duplication of mistakes. By doing this, associates are empowered to learn from others while reducing the overall risk to the organization.

Most people confuse problems with symptoms of the problem. Ask someone to describe an issue, and they describe the impact of the issue. "My car didn't start this morning. I was late to work; I must call the mechanic, etc." In reality, the real problem isn't known at this time. Perhaps the battery died or a part malfunctioned, but until that is known, a solution cannot be determined. People are impatient and want to diagnose an issue quickly and end up guessing and allowing their biases to determine well-intentioned but wrong conclusions. This ultimately wastes time and money, wasting time on fruitless ideas while the real problem continues. Continuously "solving" the same issue means the root cause of the problem has not been addressed.

Avoiding common traps in problem-solving and change management:

- **Non-standardization of routine tasks:** Giving people too much freedom to do routine tasks inevitably creates unneeded work and tasks. Time will be wasted on unnecessary processing, adding complexity and requiring potential firefighting down the road when processes break down.

- **Confusing change with improvement:** Just because something changes doesn't mean it's progress. In a worst-case scenario, the change can set us back instead of moving us forward. Making a process or product change consumes many resources and reallocates focus and attention. Without correct guidance, employees with great intentions will unintentionally consume hours (which equals dollars) and budgets on ideas that don't measurably move the organization forward. Well-known product failures like "New Coke" and "Crystal Pepsi" are great examples. Marketing and production dollars went into these ideas while ultimately hurting the brand and removing focus from the company objectives.

- **Not assessing if change is needed:** New processes involve a considerable investment of time to retrain employees and audit the new process. Before making any changes, ask how well the need for change is understood. Does the change measurably improve the current state to justify the financial and time investment? Determine how success will be measured *before* initiating a project and ensure the goal is realistic and attainable.

• **Not asking the right questions:** Asking questions throughout any change process will ensure time and money are not wasted. Employees who are heavily invested in a change project will feel compelled to find ways to justify the resource commitment. Educating staff on distinguishing change versus improvement will prevent unnecessary resource waste. Just because you can doesn't mean you should.

• **Not understanding the difference between efficiency and effectiveness:** If the main objective is to increase efficiency, the focus is on waste reduction. The goal is to minimize costs, process steps, and waste while maintaining the current quality level. You can also aim to increase quality with less waste, costs, or process steps. On the other hand, striving for effectiveness means reducing variation. Can the process deliver the same exact result each time the process is run? It entails ensuring consistent processes, aiming for higher accuracy, faster speed, simplifying complexity, and enhancing flexibility while maintaining the current level of efficiency (time and effort).

Does the team understand the concept of process drift, tracking it, and adjusting for it? Process drift is defined as a subtle but continuous process change over time, including the shared understanding of the process steps and reasoning behind the shift. New members come into a team, or new experiences start to change the original intent or definition of previously agreed upon definitions.

Issues that create process drift:

- Setting targets or standards with little thought to how much variation might be expected
- Unclear or changing expectations
- Introduction of new team members
- Change in the business environment
- Unspoken "rules"

Tracking variation gives you a baseline on what is "normal" and when things have begun to slip. Keep in mind there are both predictable and unpredictable variables. Are you prepared for both? Risk analysis can help identify both to prepare contingency plans.

A common mistake teams make is building a process without considering its scalability. Complex or fragile processes with numerous workarounds are inadvertently built to meet only one specific task and quickly break when any change is necessary. Thinking about the effect of doubling the work on a process is an easy way to test the scalability and robustness of the process.

(17) Silent Facilitation

There are countless books and advice on how to run a productive meeting. Most offer standard guidance, such as having a clear agenda with objectives, sticking to the allotted time, and, if possible, ending the meeting early. Some go one step further with advice on rules of engagement to keep the meeting running smoothly and respectfully. While most of the advice is sound in theory, it does not guarantee a highly productive and innovative session.

Meetings often fail when roles remain undefined or are improvised on the spot. To ensure productivity, it's crucial for everyone to grasp the meeting's purpose and their specific roles within it. This is especially vital in brainstorming or problem-solving sessions, demanding proactive definition and execution of roles before the meeting kicks off.

In many routine meetings, a designated facilitator is absent, and the responsibilities fall on a team leader or project owner along with the participants. Both team leaders and participants serve as subject matter experts, aligning their focus with the goals and tasks essential for meeting objectives or adhering to deadlines. Establishing clarity in roles beforehand lays the foundation for effective collaboration and goal attainment during the meeting.

A group may benefit from introducing a facilitator into a meeting if the objective is to force broader perspectives from subject matter experts concerned they may be unable to think outside the box. This happens due to natural biases, past experiences, and exposure to information. It is easier for an external facilitator to help us move past our natural tendencies and biases into a broader perspective.

Whenever possible, avoid having a subject matter expert as a facilitator. While this feels counterintuitive, there are many advantages to having someone unfamiliar with the topic. A facilitator lacking in-depth knowledge of the topic is compelled to engage the team through questioning, objective data gathering, and attentive observation of body language and verbal cues. Collaborating with the team or project leader, they define meeting goals and objectives, ensuring comprehensive preparation of the entire team for the upcoming event. The facilitator takes charge of reviewing the list of participants, ensuring a diverse array of knowledge and experience in the room. Additionally, they are adept at providing requisite training on techniques when needed, managing meeting logistics, and ensuring strict adherence to the agenda and ground rules.

For problem-solving meetings, a dedicated facilitator proves indispensable. Whether intentional or subconscious, hidden agendas often lurk among attendees. Pre-existing meetings or personal biases may subtly guide discussions towards particular topics or solutions. Inadvertent comments can derail a session, transforming it from a productive endeavor into one fraught with frustration and unproductive behaviors. A skilled facilitator anticipates and skillfully manages these dynamics, fostering an environment conducive to effective problem-solving.

A technique called "brain swarming," pioneered by Dr. Tony McCaffrey[13], who studies the science of innovation, is highly effective in minimizing dysfunctional meetings. The premise is simple: limit talking to a minimum and guide the group to brainstorm in various categories simultaneously and silently. There are three elements to this guided method. The goals the team wants to achieve will be at the top of a whiteboard (virtual or physical). At the bottom of the whiteboard will be a category for resources available. As the team begins to create its resource inventory while glancing at the objectives at the top, solutions will start to emerge. As they do, the solutions will be entered into the middle of the whiteboard until there are connections between the resources available (or desired) and the objects to be met.

Brain Swarming Example

Improve Employee Training

Sub Goals

Develop Standard Materials	Audit Skills And Mastery	Create Knowledge Base

Potential Solutions

Online Courses	LMS, SOP, Videos, PowerPoint, Demos	Certifications Skill Audits	Database	Content Experts

Resources Available

Software: Microsoft Office, LMS, Video Recording	Teaching Techniques: Demos, Lectures, Video	Subject Matter Experts

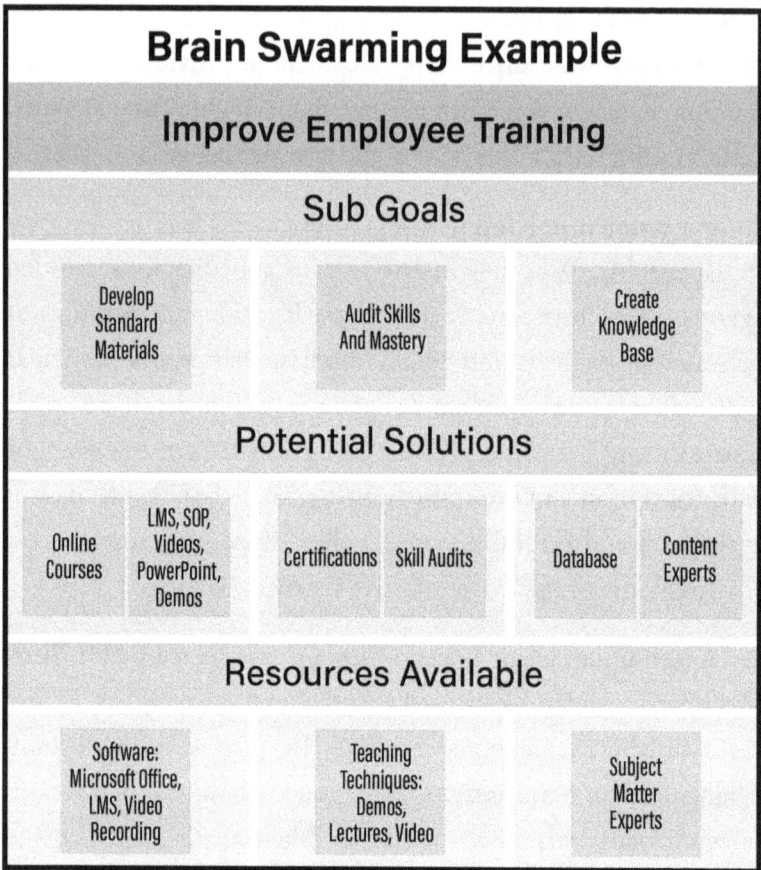

The brilliance of using this silent method for problem-solving is that limiting conversation gives little opportunity for comments that might stifle other people's ideas. By doing it simultaneously using Post-it notes (virtual or physical), other people's ideas gain visibility to add to or enhance the concept without interruption. Conversations are limited to clarifying questions or statements throughout the exercise.

As a facilitator, when categories in the solutions begin to emerge, record these categories on the whiteboard and invite participants to continue to add ideas. These exercises move remarkably quickly, with volumes of highly productive ideas within an hour. The rest of the time can then be used to prioritize the solutions for cost effectiveness, time and effort required, etc. Discussion after a brain swarming tends to be more effective as all ideas are posted without initial censorship and create a broader scope of solutions.

A variation can also be applied when a process map is required. Instead of three main categories, ask all participants to stand in the order they believe they fall in the process of being mapped. With Post-it notes in hand, ask the team to begin mapping their individual processes. Conversations are limited to the people to the left or right of them for clarification purposes as they do the exercise. Encourage teams to go into deeper dives of the processes to understand the nuances of the work. The more details that are known, the better the solution will be.

Finally, transition all whiteboards to an electronic format, allowing for easy sharing and reference as required. While I still advocate for physical exercises in a room as the optimal choice for initiating ideation and mapping, translating to an electronic format ensures that remote employees or those not physically present can promptly access and review the team's work.

(18) Enhancing Team And Data Performance Through Calibration

Routine calibration and equipment maintenance are standard practices essential to the manufacturing process. Similarly, in office environments, associates function as intellectual machines driving innovation, product development, and revenue generation.

Organizations collect thousands of data points every day that are transformed into reports used in daily decision-making and business course corrections. One of the biggest mistakes is to assume the data is correct. How often do regular maintenance and calibration of data and shared vocabulary occur? Anytime an operator collects and records data, the operator's and the data's accuracy should be regularly audited.

People are confused when I ask how often their teams are calibrated. Process drift is real, creating small but significant changes in team performance over time. The best teams continuously recalibrate, especially when they onboard new team members. Consider the following scenarios and the impact on the team dynamics, data, and culture:

- **Turnover Challenges:** When turnover occurs, the transfer of training and institutional knowledge becomes erratic, potentially jeopardizing the coherence of operations.

- **CRM Systems:** Associates select multiple categories to describe the same scenario, introducing inconsistencies and hindering accurate data interpretation.

- **Nuances in Terminology:** Changes in the nuances of meaning for common terms can lead to misunderstanding and misalignments in communication. For example, the standard of "good" varies by team member.

So, how are teams calibrated? There are several formal and informal methods to do a calibration. In the manufacturing world, there is an easy way to test the performance of machinery. It is called gage repeatability and reproducibility (gage R&R), and surprisingly, it's not difficult to adapt to a data environment.

The technique is simple:

- Take ten samples of common work in the department.

- Designate an "expert" within the group to grade the samples based on an agreed-upon rating.

- Have each member independently grade the samples of the work.

- Alter the sequence of the samples and instruct the team to regrade them one week later.

The exercise has various objectives:

- Determine the variation between the team members' final "grades" and those of the "expert." Calculate the percent of accuracy.

- Determine the overall accuracy of the team against the "expert" grade.

- Finally, see if the team members can give the same "grades" to all the samples a week later. Are they in agreement with their own initial evaluations?

The exercise can be repeated as necessary until the team is confident they will have little variation in completing the activity. Teams take several months to achieve this level of calibration, and it is a great tool to help new team members understand what is expected of them.

Another example can be applied to any situation where a CRM system or database has drop-down selections. One of the biggest assumptions made is that all associates will select the same drop-down categories for the same scenario. The reality is this is rarely the case. Most systems, in an attempt to be all-encompassing, will have too many options and leave it to the associate's discretion to select the right choice. Over time, the same scenario will appear categorized in different ways. The implications are alarming. "Major" issues become hidden in different data categories, making the full impact hard to see. Data will be skewed, and worse, decisions will be made or *not* made based on this information.

The categories used in a drop-down menu will be referred to as a disposition for simplicity. In most situations, there is a hierarchical series of drop-down menus to categorize data or a scenario, like the reason for a customer call. It is, therefore, very important to test and measure the variance in the dispositions for a selected scenario. Remember, every agent has valuable data on variance.

Several factors contribute to the variability in dispositions. Frequently, drop-down selections become overcrowded with obsolete choices. Dispositions lack intuitiveness, are often ambiguous, and may be labeled in multiple ways, leading to an unclear path for selection. Insufficient training among both new and existing associates exacerbates the issue. Without continuous calibration, disposition selections remain misaligned with the scenario.

Moreover, the forms often attempt to cater to the data needs of a broad audience, resulting in an excess of required fields and information, making the process cumbersome and prone to errors. Addressing these issues is crucial to streamline and enhance the effectiveness of the disposition selection process.

Reducing Variation In Disposition Selection

Evaluate Relevance and Clarity:

- Scrutinize for relevance, clarity, and intuitiveness.
- Identify and rectify duplicates.
- Clarify the pathway to each disposition.
- Define criteria for what constitutes an unsupportable scenario.
- Enhance visibility, usage, and reporting mechanisms.
- Review and utilize a root cause checklist.
- Consider the default disposition position.
- Assess if a disposition aligns with the requirements of other departments.
- Encourage strategic use of hashtags to capture pertinent data accurately and promote flexibility.

Comprehend Reporting Requirements:

- Assess each disposition for ease of reporting.
- Examine report details to ensure comprehensive data capture.
- Verify against call drivers to enhance accuracy.

- Determine the critical data elements required for reporting.

- Reevaluate the "other" category in reports and identify trends.

Engage Stakeholders:

- Consult with all stakeholders to ascertain their specific needs.

- Ensure that disposition selections align with the diverse requirements of each stakeholder group.

Communication and Training of Associates

- Utilize the right communication tools.

- Create surveys to test potential disposition scenarios as training material.

- Train new agents on the importance and use of disposition.

- Use a Call Coach training to include important communication methods—email versus chat.

Implementing these measures will contribute to a more standardized and effective disposition selection process, reducing variations and ensuring accurate and relevant data capture. Clear and concise disposition paths lead to a 100 percent selection rate by tech agents.

I've effectively employed the following procedure to conduct gage R&R in a call center:

1. Survey Development:

    a. Create a survey featuring three call scenarios, prompting agents to populate drop-down options as they would during an actual call.

b. Administer approximately twenty call scenarios over a span of six to eight weeks, ensuring team completion. Surveys can be seamlessly integrated between customer calls to minimize impact.

c. Surveys need not be overly intricate; they can range from a quick one-question chat survey to a more comprehensive version, depending on the context.

d. Keep the survey open-ended, requiring agents to copy the drop-down labels into the survey.

e. Expect initial wide variances, particularly during the first few iterations.

f. On average, anticipate a completion time of approximately nine minutes per survey for tech agents, contingent on the complexity and content of bonus questions.

2. Follow-Up Transparency:

a. Send a follow-up email summarizing the results and conclusions.

b. Organize a stand-up meeting to discuss observations and collaboratively draw conclusions from the survey results.

c. Be transparent by sharing analytics of survey questions and relevant data links, if applicable.

d. Include follow-up training and suggestions for the team.

e. Encourage open discussion to understand any identified wide discrepancies.

3. Visibility Maintenance:

    a. Counter the challenge of drop-down dispositions losing visibility by creating a mind map to track all dispositions visually.

4. Defined Process Implementation:

    a. Develop a structured process for adding, removing, or altering future dispositions.

    b. The lack of a defined process can lead to clutter and compromise data quality for future reporting.

By following this systematic approach, organizations can conduct effective gage R&R in a call center, ensuring clarity in disposition selection, valuable insights from surveys, and a streamlined process for ongoing improvement.

(19) Maximizing Efficiency And Team Alignment With The Pareto Principle

The Pareto principle, commonly known as the 80/20 rule, states that 80 percent of the outcomes are a result of 20 percent of the causes.[14] This disparity or imbalance can be seen almost everywhere and is especially prevalent in the workplace and personal lives.

Reflecting on the past decade, I am always amazed at the profound impact of small defects, components, or misunderstandings. A dead car battery can cause a car not to start, triggering a ripple effect throughout the day. This may result in being late to work or missing an important appointment. Malcolm Gladwell explores a strategy in his book *The Bomber Mafia*,[15] which discusses an attempt during

WWII to target manufacturing companies producing ball bearings as part of a broader strategy to secure victory. The reasoning behind this tactic lies in recognizing ball bearings as seemingly small yet indispensable components in nearly every manufacturing process. The premise is that producing various war-supporting products would become practically impossible without ball bearings.

I have seen the Pareto principle in effect in hundreds of processes. I have learned to look for it and guide employees to dive deep into their data to find it. Often, the payoff is huge. One bad ingredient can ruin a good meal. That doesn't mean the recipe or cooking process is at fault. In observing teams and management, there is a tendency to assume *everything* is broken and *everything* needs to be analyzed. This can be time-consuming and resource-intensive. Spending some time looking at all the process inputs and looking for potential quality issues can allow for a more targeted data discovery. In my experience, small but not obvious issues have often created dramatic firefighting.

A particularly noteworthy example stems from a manufacturing plant grappling with a seemingly small but costly problem. The powder paint coating was chipping off less than one percent of their products. Initial investigations targeted the usual suspects—the paint supplier, the painting process, and so on. However, justifying substantial changes was challenging, with less than one percent presenting the issue. Delving deeper into the data, they pinpointed the team responsible for the issues and, impressively, even identified the specific hour when it occurred—the lunch hour.

As it turned out, the team enjoyed having lunch together. On days they returned late, causing the materials to spend too much time in the chemicals, the paint wouldn't adhere properly throughout the rest of the manufacturing process. This several-hundred-thousand-dollar issue was ingeniously resolved by adjusting the lunch break times.

Let's pause to reflect on how the Pareto principle manifests in both our personal and professional realms. Consider the number of family members, friends, and coworkers with whom you engage in meaningful daily or weekly interactions. Deliberate on those individuals whom you actively prioritize for communication and coordination of activities. When you convert this number into a percentage relative to those you consider close, the realization might be surprising—revealing a smaller circle of active engagement despite our best intentions.

In the workplace, employees naturally interact with a limited number of individuals crucial to their work or from whom they seek advice. While this is not inherently negative, it prompts us to question its impact on team goals and overall productivity. Are there perspectives or information not actively sought that merit more attention? This includes engaging with teams possessing diverse viewpoints that could enrich experiences and understanding.

Understanding how employees allocate their time is a pivotal component of an operational excellence program. It shapes the perspectives shared within the team. Recent research from behavioral and organizational psychology experts, such as Nir Eyal, indicates that filling time with mindless tasks may provide a sense of productivity but can be counterproductive to achieving overarching goals.[16] Teams must consciously prioritize and manage time spent on critical work rather than leaving it to chance.

Consider how often teams procrastinate on tasks that, when eventually addressed, require significantly less effort than initially perceived. Tasks pivotal to project progression or capable of altering the trajectory may have been postponed in favor of "low-hanging fruit" and the allure of quick wins that, while providing a sense of productivity, do not substantially impact the project.

20 Using Kano Analysis To Unlock Customer Requirements

I often ask product managers and engineers about their confidence in creating a product or service aligned with the customer's desires. I remind them of the cost of mistakes in terms of money and time, not to mention opportunity costs. I am typically presented with a list of features. I question how they know whether customers want or are willing to pay for these features. Features are not customer requirements. The methodology used is often limited to surveys or a small group of beta customers. A few customers who may or may not accurately represent our target customer base influence the full customer experience. In certain instances, there is a lack of effort to incorporate the voice of the customer, and changes are driven solely by managerial opinions.

Let me highlight the danger of not building an understanding or good customer requirements with a familiar scenario. I ask people to imagine they are given $100,000 to spend on a car. They are then taken to a dealership and asked, "What can I show you?" From pick-up trucks to SUVs to sports cars, people typically describe the color, size of the engine, or comfort features they are looking for in their next vehicle. Then I asked, "Why didn't you ask for no paint damage, four tires, a steering wheel, and an engine?" Everyone laughs, and the answer is universally the same: *that's expected.*

"That's expected." Here lies the root of many missed opportunities in feature or service creation. The problem with *that's expected* lives in the fact that it is also *unspoken*. Hundreds of hours are spent conducting voice-of-the-customer surveys and analysis to determine what a customer wants, but they won't give the elements critical to its success. Customers don't mention them because it's expected and assumed you already know and understand.

In 2018, Apple launched the iPhone X with an odd software bug. The phone was having problems answering phones. The *Financial Times* reported that hundreds of owners complained on Apple forums about the issue, quoting one user as saying, "Whenever I receive an incoming call in my iPhone X, ringtones start, but the display comes in after six to eight seconds." Another wrote, "I can often not see an incoming call coming, can only hear it. At other times, there is a significant delay."

A cell phone's obvious, expected feature is the ability to answer a phone quickly. The experience of spending nearly a thousand dollars for a phone that couldn't answer phone calls must have been a huge disappointment for hundreds of customers who expected the quality to be much better. A consumer's expected service, product, and feature performance cannot easily change with additional features. Giving a customer a hundred more apps to install on their phone for free would not likely satisfy a user who wants the incoming call bug to be fixed.

This is why understanding the principles of Kano analysis is essential. At its core, Kano is deceptively simple. It breaks all features into three categories: expected, satisfier, or delighter. Expected features are features that the product or service needs to get right. These features don't come out in surveys, so identify them through *painstorming*. Review warranties and customer complaints to understand what customers expect to build the right services in the future.

Satisfiers are what show up in surveys. The more you have, the happier you are—lower prices, extra features, etc. Delighters are those items that a customer doesn't know they want until it's given to them. This is the "extra" they weren't expecting. Delighters should not be used to mask issues with expected features. Over time, delighters become satisfiers, and satisfiers become expected items. Bluetooth in cars was considered a premium option at one time but is an expected item in vehicles today.

Testing where the feature lies within the customer's expectation is relatively easy. Simply ask, "How would you feel if the product/service had _____?" Alternatively, ask, "How would you feel if the product/service *did not* have _____?" For example, "How would you feel if your new car did not have four tires?" The strength of the reaction indicates whether the feature is expected or merely nice to have.

Use this simple test to prioritize the efforts going into product designs and test the customer's desire for it. Time and money will be saved if customers realize that they might find it nice to have but are unwilling to spend more money on it.

21 Why Email Is An Ineffective Tool For Managing Work

While the purpose of emails is to communicate information, the effectiveness of this communication method is often questionable. Staff and executives often share concerns over the overwhelming number of emails they receive.

"Are they effective?" The answer is usually "no." Emails are frequently overlooked, misunderstood, or left unread as they become buried in crowded inboxes. How will reports or policy changes be stored for future reference when sending out reports or policy changes? When it comes to storing important reports or policy changes sent via email, recipients are left to devise their own organizational systems, leading to inconsistent compliance with instructions or changes in policy or procedure. Key metrics and reports are better served by implementing dashboards that everyone visibly sees. Sharing information publicly can also bring to light bigger issues and allow teams to find solutions.

Employees often resort to using email not as a means of productivity but as a form of procrastination. It's a great way to buy additional time when they anticipate a slow response from the recipient. How often do you hear "I sent an email" as a response to whether or not a task was completed? Even worse, when a reply doesn't come, they state, "It's been two weeks; I will follow up." Two weeks wasted and many more to come. If the task were truly important, a follow-up phone call or visit would have moved the task forward.

Determine the underlying purpose behind your emails and explore alternative solutions. For quick queries demanding immediate responses, consider using chat platforms. A centralized repository like SharePoint, followed by a group meeting, can be more effective for announcements or tasks requiring action. This approach facilitates easy information retrieval based on categories or topics. In the case of routine reports, establish a central repository and share links, guiding staff to a consistent location for information retrieval, thereby reducing the burden of managing overflowing inboxes.

Central repositories, governed by retention policies, offer better control and ensure information remains up-to-date. This approach minimizes the risk of outdated information stored in individual inboxes, preventing potential issues.

CHAPTER 7

The Technology Strategy

(22) How Technology Misleads Us

Over the past two decades, introducing new technologies in the workplace has brought unexpected challenges. Typically, the responsibility and associated costs of this task are delegated to specific employees with biases toward particular software rather than following a structured process to assess new software against corporate strategies. Over time, this can become a burden for IT, requiring support and maintenance or creating a single point of failure when employees with institutional knowledge depart. It's crucial to consider how technology is integrated into a corporate environment without excessively limiting the creativity and flexibility of the team.

While organizations invest significant time in crafting strategic objectives, KPIs, and a vision for what they aim to achieve, little guidance is provided to various departments regarding the technology used to realize these goals. When was the last time the organization assessed the entire technology stack from a strategic perspective, developing a strategy for when and how technology should be employed? How many elements of the company's technology stack have redundant features?

In 2019, MySpace admitted that millions of audio clips, videos, and photos uploaded before 2015 were likely lost during a botched server migration.[17] This, of course, was an accident. Data loss is not always unintended. Consider the evolution from VHS to DVDs and then streaming—technological advancements often lead to obsolescence, and content or data can be lost in the migration. Organizations must acknowledge and plan for this as technology strategies are devised.

Over time, the presence of corporate silos and mishandled information leads to the emergence of numerous "productivity" tools. Each software solution pledges to achieve the elusive goal of seamless data integration and management. However, these tools frequently connect disparate data and information streams from various sources in a haphazard manner, complicating the quest for a fully integrated system. Instead of achieving a smooth flow of information throughout the organization, interruptions and hesitations occur at different points, causing confusion among external customers and internal departments.

How did we get here? One of the reasons is the promise these tools make to organize data. An assortment of technologies is implemented to find meaning in the sea of information and end up obscuring the important trends. These feature-rich tools frequently overlap in functionalities, resulting in duplication of calendar, chat, and document storage features. With teams selecting different document repositories, locating materials and information may turn into a scavenger hunt or simply be missed during the execution of a workflow. Another risk is that business needs will quickly outpace the original capacity of the software. This places the organization at the mercy of the software vendor and their "feature request" list. This dependency can greatly affect flexibility and costs in the long run. Teach employees to think strategically about every purchase, collaborate with other teams with similar needs, and build requirements with a long-term perspective.

Do you experience the following?

- Departments that don't "talk" to each other, so customer information isn't easily shared between them.

- Customer data is maintained in several software databases, with no easy way to get 365-degree views of all of it.

- Multiple calendars for the same teams.

- Multiple ways of sharing the same information across teams (chats, email, phone, meetings).

Collaborative efforts naturally move information into more shared areas. Across teams, a proliferation of unstructured data (data that cannot be easily queried or contained across multiple platforms) has created significant challenges in visibility and information management. Consider the impact on various aspects:

Calendars—A multitude of calendars not visible to everyone on the team or across the organization.

- Pro—a multitude of calendars for various purposes.

- Con—Important dates are scattered, leading to missed deadlines.

- Con—Important documents embedded within calendar invites are difficult to locate over time.

File Sharing—Documents contained in personal and network folders such as Box, Sync.com, SharePoint, Basecamp, Google Docs, Microsoft Office suite, Dropbox, GitHub (code repositories), USB drives, etc.

- Pro—Easy storage and sharing across platforms.

- Con—Documents containing corporate intellectual property are not properly secured.

- Con—Terminated employees may still have access, risking data breaches.

- Con—Documents and information can be lost or forgotten over time.

Video Conferencing—Skype, Zoom, Microsoft Teams, WhatsApp, etc. Videoconferencing has replaced meetings.

- Pro—Meetings can be recorded by those not in attendance for future viewing.

- Pro—If recorded, meetings can generate and share transcripts.

- Con—Unless an audio transcript is shared, most information contained will be lost. If chat is being used, where are the chat transcripts kept?

- Con—If the transcript is shared via email, there is no central repository to go back and review notes.

Process Mapping/Mind Mapping—Xmind, MindMeister, Microsoft Visio, EA, and cloud-based mind-mapping tools.

- Pro—Organizes problems, resources, relationships, and solutions.
- Con—Often limited to addressing a specific problem and quickly becomes outdated.

CRM/Ticketing—Jira, Microsoft, Salesforce

- Pro—Contains customer-company interactions.
- Con—Information can become siloed and relies on good notes and disposition selection from the agents using it.
- Con—Can quickly become bloated with excess data and difficult to extract "clean" data.

Enterprise Resource Planning (ERP) Systems

- Pro—Contains basic data needs such as customer account and history information.
- Con—Data contained in an ERP system can be duplicated across multiple systems.

Project Management—Asana, Monday.com, Wrike, ActiveCollab, Microsoft Project

- Pro—Can be used to keep track of all project deadlines and requirements.
- Con—Can create data silos.

Presentation Apps—PowerPoint, Prezi, Google Slides, SlideDog, Visme, Adobe, Canva, Powtoon (animation)

- Pro—Can be used to create visual representations of data and information.

- Con—Can create data silos when the data contained in the presentation is not easily accessible to all stakeholders. Data is often kept only by the creator.

- Con—Data is not queriable.

Time Tracking/Resource Management—HR software, time tracking

- Pro—Can be used to assign time allocated to projects.

- Con—This is usually not connected to project management systems, so it's difficult to fully understand the amount of time being lost on stalled projects.

Kanban boards/Work boards/Whiteboards—Electronic boards (Trello, Zoom, Miro, Mural)

- Pro—Helps organize team ideas, workflow, or project artifacts.

- Con—Lack of organizational visibility may blindside other teams by changes in work requirements, decisions, etc.

Chat Apps— (Zoom, WhatsApp, Skype, Messenger, WeChat, etc.)

- Pro—Easy to use; it fosters a greater ability for people to communicate.

- Cons—Many software programs include a chat application. This creates silos when information doesn't flow to all stakeholders not included in these informal chats. Some chats disappear—such as chats contained during Zoom meetings.

Standing Meetings—Fifteen-minute daily or weekly check-ins

- Pro—Provides for quick team check-ins.

- Con—Lacks notes captured or reviewed. There are countless complaints from employees that they were excluded from a meeting they should have attended, or information was not shared by someone attending.

Instead of creating a technology strategy, the common fallacy is to look for technology solutions to link disparate systems. While quick fixes like robotic process automation (e.g., Automation Anywhere or Blue Prism) and the allure of low-code solutions might seem appealing, they should be employed intentionally and not haphazardly inserted between processes. Typically, automation serves as a workaround for challenging-to-replace disparate or legacy systems.

Another common method of dealing with data is building data warehouses or using data platforms that link disparate data sets, such as PowerBI and Tableau. By combining automation with these data platforms, there is a promise to leverage data into more useful information.

A strategic vision is imperative to prevent organizations from devolving into a disjointed collection of processes optimized for specific tasks. A well-defined strategy empowers technology to create a seamless flow rather than a series of fragmented processes across various departments. Evaluate processes not merely to address specific issues but also to ascertain how they align with the broader structure of the overall organizational experience.

(23) Introducing Automation Into The Workplace

Automation encompasses a spectrum, ranging from simple macros to sophisticated scripts. As technology evolves, encourage all employees to learn and understand the various automation tools available.

Depending on the culture and average age of the organization, automation will be adopted at different levels. A younger organization may seek to automate everything, which also carries risks. When automation is introduced, there is someone's logic behind it. When business rules change, the automation becomes outdated. It performs a task perfectly even though the task may no longer be appropriate. View automation as another virtual worker that still needs to be audited. Automation left unchecked will eventually break processes.

There's a widespread misconception that automation replaces workers. In reality, automation accelerates work and rarely eliminates it. It moves processes quicker and, if not planned correctly, can bottleneck in unexpected areas. It quickly changes the nature of the work and the skill set needed. When automation is used to complete lower-task work, it creates a need for higher-end work. This shift may require a workforce with enhanced skills and potentially higher labor costs, but this is not necessarily disadvantageous. A smarter, more creative employee brings more value to the workforce. They introduce higher levels of innovation with a greater on someone who can only complete menial tasks.

Where there is hesitation in bringing automation, show employees how their work can benefit. Everyone has time-consuming tasks where automation can make a significant impact. Viewing automation as a virtual assistant changes perception and allows us to do the work we enjoy versus the monotonous functions we must complete.

How do you get started? There are many ways to introduce automation, from creating conditions and rules in Outlook to creating simple macros in Excel. Third-party simple automation scripts or macros to get us started can be purchased. Many free or open-source software provide free or low-cost productivity tools like Google or OpenAI. A little research on current software tools will highlight you are likely underutilizing. Begin with email tools, automating data entry before attempting to automate process workflows fully. By starting slow, you will gain an understanding of what should be automated, as well as what will always need human oversight.

When basic automation tools are integrated into daily tasks, introduce new tools such as low code automation solutions like Robotic Process Automation (RPA). These can be costly solutions unless you have workflows where the return on the investment makes it worth the cost.

(24) The Rise And Impact Of Shadow IT

Having worked in the software industry, I've witnessed firsthand the impact of Shadow IT—a broad term encompassing the unauthorized use of any information technology system, service, or device not formally approved or supported by the IT department. Often introduced as a workaround to the perceived or actual shortcomings of central information systems or policies, shadow IT can improve employee productivity and drive innovation. However, its use introduces serious security risks that can leave the organization exposed.

Associates normally see the benefits to their productivity and agility as a rationale for its use; they rarely understand the risks to the organization. While the IT department has diligently created cybersecurity solutions or protocols, the introduction of shadow IT can quickly render all of these precautions useless. A nontechnical associate can rarely assess cloud workloads and services developers use for serious vulnerabilities, such as default passwords or misconfigurations.

The Gartner Group predicts that one-third of successful attacks will come through shadow IT resources.[18] But exactly what does shadow IT look like? It can be as simple as purchasing productivity applications or cloud services that fall below the purchasing thresholds outlined by IT. Or it could involve bringing in personal devices and creating personal accounts on document-sharing accounts to store or move company-related information.

Here are some examples of shadow IT I have seen or heard about throughout the years:

- Employees install non-enterprise-sanctioned chat apps such as WhatsApp and transfer sensitive intellectual property files through it.

- Employees create their own personal accounts on cloud-based software, such as collaborative whiteboards, project management, or document-sharing services. Passwords and access to sensitive files are unknown and not managed by the company.

- Employees store sensitive information on personal storage accounts from physical hard drives to cloud storage with limited cybersecurity protocols.

Ultimately, the root causes of the proliferation are system inefficiencies in policies and infrastructure. When an organization fails to provide the associate with adequate resources to complete their work, they will turn to external resources. Perhaps the organization has made procuring resources so costly and labor-intensive (months of vetting, budget proposals, review processes) that circumventing established processes is tempting and easier. It's not uncommon to have limited IT resources and staff, and when coupled with high levels of administration and bureaucracy, associates find it easier to find their own solutions.

As teams generate solutions, they inadvertently establish silos, hindering the establishment of a unified data source. This fragmentation poses challenges to achieving a comprehensive and accurate data analysis. Individual accounts remain inaccessible to other members within the organization. In the event of an employee departure or termination, there is a risk of continued access to cloud-stored assets by the departing individual, potentially resulting in the business losing access to those critical resources.

Shadow IT is not subject to corporate policies and procedures, meaning data may not be backed up, archived, or encrypted in line with company policy, potentially exposing it to data theft or mismanagement. Most associates do not understand the technical details of their organization's cybersecurity solutions and don't evaluate purchased solutions to ensure they meet these requirements.

Shadow IT services rarely enforce strong credential policies, leaving them open to weak or default credentials that can be exploited and used as a pathway into the organization's broader corporate network.

While associates turn to shadow IT to reduce costs, the reality is that an enterprise solution for the entire organization may be more cost-effective than the patchwork solutions created across teams over time. It could also reduce costs indirectly in the form of noncompliance fines and penalties, reputational harm in the event of a breach, or timely and intensive IT support if and when the service needs to be migrated or de-provisioned.

The challenge of reducing shadow IT lies not with employees but with the business. Organizations must take steps to understand and fulfill the needs of their employees through comprehensive and regular audits. Approval processes for new resources should have low administrative overhead while monitoring all devices, applications, and systems used to conduct work. Create a security posture that enforces good security policies without creating an environment so difficult to work within that people are encouraged to work outside the system.

25 Auditing Organizational Resources

Organizations without a clearly defined technology strategy are prone to deploying numerous resources that duplicate functions. Redundancies are prevalent in various software packages, making it valuable to identify commonalities and select the optimal product for each task. Managing the intricacies of a large, globally dispersed organization presents the difficulty of efficiently sharing vital information among teams. The lack of awareness regarding existing resources and licenses requested by other teams often results in unnecessary replication of efforts. This continual reinvention of solutions leads to the adoption of multiple software tools performing similar functions. Aside from the potential financial waste in subscription costs, this practice also scatters information across diverse platforms, posing a consolidation challenge in the future.

With software solutions being quite expensive, a more cost-effective approach is to leverage licenses that can be easily expanded rather than allowing teams to explore new solutions. Understanding what is already available and vetted can allow teams to quickly enable a solution rather than assume they must go through a long bureaucratic process to get what they need.

The easiest way to begin is by conducting a simple survey on the most commonly used tools in the organization—preferred chat solution, document solution, calendar solution, etc. The objective is not only to identify common tools but also to pinpoint any solutions in use without proper authorization. If several associates in the organization bring in their own devices (tablets, second computers), reevaluate their use and whether or not it makes sense for the corporation to provide them instead.

Collaborate with the finance department to scrutinize technology expenditures, identifying existing solutions and licenses within the organization. Establish a centralized repository housing all agreements and contracts, facilitating the verification of usage limitations when necessary. Analyze help-desk requests to discern prevalent issues and common user needs. As you identify them, begin to assign a risk level to the use of the solutions as well.

Assign a risk level to identified solutions and begin the consolidation process, targeting redundancy for elimination. Prioritize resources that have undergone thorough testing and possess a readily available skill set for training purposes. Scrutinize the software's credentialing methods, distinguishing between personal and corporate credentials.

Implement educational initiatives and establish policies that promote common-sense security practices, such as refraining from using corporate email for personal activities like retail or social media. Organizations can streamline technology expenses, enhance efficiency, and fortify security protocols by taking these measures. There are several goals for this type of audit:

- Identification of potential security threats.
- Consolidation and cost reduction of products with overlapping functionalities.
- Elimination of unused software.
- Evaluation of the impact of incorporating personal devices on work productivity and security.

- Identifying gaps in technology infrastructure to meet employee needs.

- Creation of technology policies that meet cybersecurity demands while maintaining flexibility.

PART THREE

Sustaining Excellence

CHAPTER 8

Mitigating Unnecessary Risks

Today's companies are vastly complex. With hundreds of business processes operating in parallel and a diverse array of personality types and styles, it's a wonder businesses don't experience failure more often. Yet, failures occur, and unnecessary risk is introduced into daily operations without thinking. Teaching associates to evaluate risk before change is key to creating a successful process excellence program.

Consider that the term "risk" holds varied interpretations shaped by individual experiences. Some view it as an opportunity to comprehend potential challenges and devise strategies for managing or mitigating risks. Others perceive risk inherently as negative, driving them to pursue its complete elimination. The key objective, however, lies in effective risk management rather than total elimination, as excessive risk aversion may inadvertently give rise to more significant risks.

A reluctance to embrace risk could cause teams to overlook valuable opportunities in implementing ideas, partnerships, or ventures, potentially resulting in a loss of competitiveness and diminished returns. Establishing what qualifies as acceptable risk and impart techniques for evaluating and managing risk appropriately whenever feasible is crucial. By defining a balanced approach to risk, organizations can foster a culture that navigates challenges adeptly while capitalizing on opportunities for growth and innovation.

The most significant risk within any organization lies in the deployment of communication. With a growing number of remote employees, the challenge is evident in how crucial conversations that typically occur in a physical break room are conveyed to colleagues working remotely. The transition to remote work introduces the risk of small distractions leading to lapses in communication, such as forgetting to send an email or make a phone call to keep others informed.

Furthermore, failure patterns may be observed but not addressed due to challenges in navigating the political landscape. The existing business culture may discourage employees from proactively bringing up concerns, fearing negative perceptions, or being seen as not contributing to the team. Based on organizational responses to previous situations, employees are easily "trained" to omit information to avoid an uncomfortable position. This dynamic can hinder open communication and proactive problem-solving within the organization. What information, if readily understood, would change a decision in the organization?

Communication gaps are only one way risk is introduced into organizations. Several common business scenarios contribute to the introduction of risk:

- **Low Compliance on Established Procedures.** Failure to conduct regular audits to ensure that established procedures align with the expected standards. Presuming that ongoing changes have not significantly impacted operations, leading to a potential pitfall. Regularly reassessing whether standards remain accurate and proper execution is essential for effective risk management.

- **Shortened Deadlines.** Unforeseen delays such as shipping or approvals can compress a two-week deadline into three days. Several steps are cut to accommodate the new deadline. In the midst of firefighting, sacrifices may occur in areas such as quality, cost control, and seamless handoffs.

- **Evolution of an Overcomplicated Process** A simple process may evolve into a time-consuming, labor-intensive, manual process. It might have started innocently as a one-off vendor, customer, or manager request, but it is now a full-blown job. It has so many steps you're afraid to be interrupted mid-step or lose your place. There is a good chance mistakes have probably happened, but they are not severe enough (yet) to fix the process. The task should be simplified, but you can't find the time. These are referred to as workarounds.

• **Multitasking.** Multitasking, often equated with productivity, can lead to mistakes and wasted time. Studies prove people don't multitask well and are prone to making more mistakes and wasting more time in the end correcting errors (assuming they are found).[19]

• **Ineffective or Lack of Feedback Mechanisms.** Feedback mechanisms to alert you to a failure are missing until well after the failure has occurred. There is no "gas gauge," and you are unaware you need to refuel until you are stranded on the side of the road.

• **Unrealistic or Unarticulated Project Goals.** This is where a lack of proper communication affects the final outcome. Poorly defined system requirements at the project outset contribute to inaccurate estimates of needed resources such as time and money. This is then compounded by poor reporting due to many unknown variables.

• **Reworking Equals Defects.** Not only is time spent correcting work, but time is wasted in creating the unsatisfactory work in the first place. It may not seem like much, but due to the cumulative effect of reworking throughout the organization, errors get exponentially expensive to correct farther downstream. Get proactive in eliminating and preventing reworking.

• **Postponing Maintenance.** Postponing essential maintenance can have far-reaching consequences. Delaying routine maintenance and upgrades escalates minor issues into larger, more costly projects in the future. Addressing these issues promptly is critical to maintaining a healthy and sustainable operational environment. Neglecting known issues because of perceived effort results in an accumulated work backlog and contributes to higher employee turnover and the persistence of outdated processes and technologies. This situation impedes current efficiency and lays the groundwork for future challenges.

Foster a culture that encourages the constructive discussion of issues without blame. Increase the quality and speed of communication across all levels of the organization to anticipate and prevent potential issues down the road. Introduce control mechanisms such as dashboards and Key Performance Indicators (KPIs) to enable real-time corrections.

Introduce error-proofing concepts into all processes, making them robust and resistant to failure. Think of it like the spellchecker function on a word processor. No matter how fast you type, you will immediately know the accuracy of the typed text before the work is forwarded. Do your processes give this type of immediate feedback?

Rushing and complexity are great places to introduce unnecessary and costly defects and reworking to the organization. Limit multitasking to just lower tasks that have good failure mechanisms in place. Educate everyone on properly observing processes in motion with a critical eye to unnecessary risk. Utilize LEAN tools like Failure Mode and Effects Analysis (FMEA) for effective risk analysis.

Curating A Problem-Solving Library

The adage that history repeats itself until its lessons are learned holds true. Within organizations, these lessons often echo with each reorganization, employee departure, business transformation, or natural evolution. While society values documentation and history preservation, many organizations perceive these practices as time-consuming, unnecessary, or even wasteful.

The common refrain, "Does anyone remember why we did that?" underscores the critical need to transform individual knowledge into shared information to benefit organizational growth. Every change enacted within an organization originally served a rational purpose. However, in the dynamic landscape of evolving products and services, swift decision-making is often lauded and rewarded during periods of change. While change itself is not inherently negative, losing sight of the reasons behind past decisions can lead to a situation where mistakes are repeated. Maintaining a clear understanding of both our current position and future direction is crucial to avoiding such pitfalls.

One of the greatest challenges in process excellence is maintaining a comprehensive record akin to a library or history of all implemented improvements. This record measures accomplishments and provides a valuable resource for understanding the evolution of processes, features, or services. Examining the history of changes offers insights into the rationale behind decisions and facilitates a natural progression toward the next iteration. This approach minimizes the risk of duplicating research efforts, enabling seamless innovation based on prior iterations.

A well-organized library becomes essential for large organizations, allowing new and experienced associates to efficiently search through keywords and retrieve information on related activities. A robust process excellence program incorporates straightforward documentation of associates' work. In manufacturing plants, this might manifest as suggestion cards posted on corkboards or, in some cases, stored in simple databases. However, there is often a lack of a formalized structure to organize and connect these valuable "ideas."

Establishing a program with straightforward documentation and database integration empowers organizations to harness all employees' collective work and creativity over an extended period. A practical approach involves adapting a commonly used LEAN project tracking tool, such as the A3 form, into a database format. Encouraging all employees to complete this form before concluding a project ensures comprehensive documentation. Email workflows simplify communication, automatically alerting relevant managers about ongoing ideas and activities. Whatever system is employed, it should facilitate filtering, searching, and creating different views. Enhancing usability can be achieved through category creation and the use of hashtags for efficient searching. Platforms in TEAMS or Monday.com with integrated email workflows for status notifications prove effective for this purpose.

To fully capitalize on the knowledge acquired from classes or improvement projects, it is imperative to establish a robust tracking system that fosters the sharing of ideas and accomplishments. Use a method that allows every employee to create their entries easily and simply and allows you to do quick searches, filtering, and aggregating data. Consistent documentation, active collaboration, and monthly reviews of team projects instill a habitual awareness of improvement opportunities among the organization's members.

When I do tours of other companies, a common mistake I observe is the use of physical documentation only. In manufacturing companies, the common method is to have employees fill out a physical card with their ideas and implementation plan. While this makes sense because most employees are not in front of a computer, by not translating these into a digital database, the ideas and evolution of processes cannot be reviewed or leveraged. Documentation in physical forms is usually thrown away or filed but rarely looked at again. In today's world, there are many ways to electronically store these ideas so they can be queried later as a way to see how processes have changed.

Mandating team members to document yearly improvements instills a proactive mindset, prompting them to actively seek opportunities for enhancement in their daily tasks. Underlining the significance of this effort, it becomes an integral part of their performance review. To bolster their journey, organizations should champion continuous learning and training, encompassing both job-related skills and problem-solving techniques. Encouraging a culture of perpetual improvement involves challenging teams to view their daily work through a fresh lens. Here are a few questions designed to prompt this shift in perspective:

• "Is this truly the best way to perform this task?" This simple question creates a moment of reflection, fostering proactive problem-solving in their daily work.

- What prevents you from reducing the time to do this task by 90%?

- Is this process a workaround? Can the task be streamlined with current technologies?

Making it a requirement has many benefits:

- Employees take ownership of identifying problems and proposing solutions.

- Employees challenge each other to improve products and processes.

- A culture of requirement promotes open discussions on challenging or sensitive subjects.

- Ideas are swiftly vetted, and funding can be allotted when needed.

- Improvement projects originate from every part of the organization—from facilities to senior management.

- Small improvements often lead to larger-scale improvement projects.

- All employees consistently contribute to problem-solving, fostering ongoing learning and skill development.

Creating A Culture Of Continuous Learning And Sharing

Embracing continuous learning becomes an essential approach for every team member when addressing process failures. Encouraging the team to consistently question "why" catalyzes refining their inquiries. These thoughtful questions lead to profound discoveries, sparking inventive solutions and ultimately driving improved outcomes. The positive shifts in group dynamics resulting from these enhanced results contribute to an improved organizational culture and performance. The upgraded group dynamics attract high-quality employees, prompting a shift in hiring criteria to seek similarly curious individuals, thereby reinforcing the culture of continuous improvement.

Create an environment that nurtures continuous learning as an ongoing journey. Support and motivate employees to pursue certifications, attend industry events, and participate in collaborative learning initiatives. A culture of perpetual learning equips teams to adapt to evolving demands and contribute innovative solutions effectively.

Establishing a culture of process excellence holds little value if the knowledge acquired is not effectively applied. It's crucial to assess what an individual has learned and what new insights have emerged from the improvement process. The focus should be on transforming this knowledge into actionable information to guide others facing similar challenges.

Knowing is not the same as doing. Do you engage in job training or job coaching? The distinction between merely instructing someone on performing a job and actively demonstrating specific work techniques can elevate an employee from a mediocre contributor to a highly productive one. While considerable emphasis is placed on the inherent abilities an employee brings to the job, the process used to train and integrate them into the organization's culture should not be overlooked. Although there may be a substantial gap between poor and good performers, robust processes can help mitigate some of these challenges.

In the book *Building Organizational Fitness*, Ryuji Fukuda estimates the difference between a poor-performing frontline employee and a high-level one is around 20 percent. The difference between mid- and top-level management can be up to 1,000 percent. This means a poor-performing manager can make an organization ten times worse.[20]

An operational excellence program is a dynamic process requiring active engagement from all staff departments for company-wide improvements. This initiative promotes ongoing awareness and improvement in daily work, providing a structured approach to integrate knowledge and experience, thereby enhancing the creativity and innovation of the entire organization. Positive reinforcement in various forms is essential for widespread adoption.

Ensuring the seamless and rapid flow of data, information, and knowledge throughout the organization is critical as part of this process. Leveraging technology and information capabilities enables the transformation of this knowledge into effective decision-making and sustained applied innovation. A curated problem-solving library is a valuable tool for documenting gained knowledge, but its effectiveness relies on regular consultation.

An excellent organization mirrors excellence in an individual: open-minded and eager to learn. Organizations can cultivate learning through diverse methods, ranging from book groups and improvement project study groups to evaluating best practices for wider dissemination. Employing various communication methods, such as employee meetings, courses in a Learning Management System (LMS), or targeted group presentations, ensures continuous sharing and creates an expectation for exposure to new internal or external ideas.

Learning Management Systems (LMS) should be integral to a process excellence program. Despite advancements in services and offerings, teaching and training methods often lag behind. While procedures outline basic job steps, demonstrating or teaching job techniques is equally crucial. Alongside the database of explanations, incorporating various learning techniques is vital. Unfortunately, even in progressive organizations, experiences of stagnant PowerPoint presentations, trainers assigned by default, and disorganized lesson plans are not uncommon.

Ongoing sharing and learning within the organization are essential for establishing and sustaining a process excellence program that delivers substantial returns. Organizational commitment holds true significance when effectively communicated and put into practice. Slogans, motivational talks, and meetings have limited impact over time and are not designed to achieve much in isolation.

How To Acknowledge And Recognize Employee Contributions

They say that genuine attention is a powerful gift to offer someone else. While it's a common instinct to commend employees for a job well done, praise isn't about the individual but the judgment the praise-giver imparts. This can sometimes evoke discomfort, suspicion, or the unpleasant feeling of being judged. Psychologist Carol Dweck and her team at Columbia studied the effect of praise on students in a dozen New York schools.[21] Children labeled as "smart," something beyond their control, were less inclined to exert effort, became risk-averse, and tended to focus more on image maintenance. Excessive praise can diminish performance, encourage cheating, and hinder the development of resilience and perseverance learned from mistakes.

If praise isn't the solution, what should one do? Instead of praising someone's work, it's more beneficial to specifically acknowledge their work without passing judgment. Rather than telling someone how wonderful their work was, acknowledge the merits, such as timely completion or achieving performance targets. A proper acknowledgment allows the recipient to agree with the statement and signals that someone is paying attention to their efforts. By specifically highlighting the details of someone's work and performance, recognition reinforces behaviors and actions.

To enhance effectiveness, acknowledge individuals publicly, whether in team meetings or other forums provided by the company. Acknowledge actual accomplishments, be specific about the actions taken and the results produced, and focus on completed tasks rather than just ideas. Avoid adjectives that imply judgment. While praise is given, ensure there is a pause between the acknowledgment and the praise.

How employees are recognized is a crucial aspect of establishing an operational excellence culture. We utilized best practice sharing meetings to acknowledge and share the exceptional work of our teams, serving as a guide for others interested in improving performance and understanding what the organization values.

Be cautious not to foster a competitive environment when thanking and recognizing employees. In our organization, we assigned points to completed continuous improvement (CI) projects for the entire team, which could be redeemed for merchandise or other rewards. The point system, rather than a competitive ranking, allows individuals to concentrate on the work itself rather than the prizes. It serves as a thank-you for their contribution without making them feel judged against the work of others.

Into The Future Of CI

Establishing a culture, rather than just a continuous improvement program, is pivotal for determining the company's long-term success beyond the program itself. A well-crafted culture of continuous improvement has the potential to permeate every facet of the organization.

Recruiting employees who actively contribute to the organization's success is not merely important; it is crucial for the organization to survive and thrive Having individuals at every process juncture who not only care but are personally invested in the organization's success is the foundation of great companies.

Fortunately, the right people are likely already in place. Employees with toxic attitudes and behaviors will become conspicuous as the culture transforms. Those who resist embracing improvement will likely self-select out of the group over time as the cultural shift progresses. How these individuals are managed will set the tone for the entire organization. Tolerating the status quo is not an option; instead, a commitment to embracing improvement is paramount. Assume that employees are eager to get started and showcase their talents—an operational excellence program is their opportunity to shine.

Understanding and acknowledging biases is essential for personal success and the success of any cultural transformation. Cultivating comfort with being proven wrong and adopting an attitude of continuous learning facilitates an easier acceptance of challenges.

Acknowledge that human biases pose a significant impediment to achieving success, particularly when it comes to the challenge of disengaging from projects where substantial time or financial resources have already been invested. Opting for a fresh start might be more cost-effective than attempting to salvage a project. For executives, admitting mistakes and steering in a new direction can be discomforting, as it involves overcoming loss aversion. This potent emotion assigns greater value to things with a sense of ownership.

Examine the initiatives that your organization rewards. A common oversight lies in the persistent pursuit of new features or services in an attempt to keep a product or service "fresh." Frequently, customers express a preference for the existing features to function better or more seamlessly. This sentiment is often echoed by employees, puzzled by the organization's choice to allocate resources to create new features rather than addressing known issues or bugs.

A striking example of this occurred recently with the popular game Fortnite. In November 2023, the game decided to return to its original Chapter 1 map. Witnessing the profound excitement and the resurgence of gaming activities among my little boy and his friends, who had taken an eighteen-month hiatus from the game, highlighted the impact of returning to familiar and beloved elements. This experience underscores the point that customers don't always desire constant and perplexing changes to their phone apps, software, or services. Learning curves associated with relocated features or alterations are not always welcomed.

———————————— ▽ ————————————

Customers don't always desire constant and perplexing changes to their phone apps, software, or services. Learning curves associated with relocated features or alterations are not always welcomed.

———————————— △ ————————————

A poignant comment from an executive resonates in this context: "We paid for that." This statement emphasizes the significant investment in development, marketing, and sales costs associated with a product or feature that, in reality, may not be what customers truly desire or are willing to pay for. Recognizing the value in refining existing features and addressing customer needs, rather than incessantly introducing new elements, can lead to more meaningful and appreciated advancements.

———————————— ▽ ————————————

Recognizing the value in refining existing features and addressing customer needs, rather than incessantly introducing new elements, can lead to more meaningful and appreciated advancements.

———————————— △ ————————————

Within the realm of continuous improvement initiatives, the conventional emphasis often gravitates towards addition or substitution. Yet, it is crucial not to underestimate the profound value inherent in subtraction—the deliberate removal of tasks, features, services, or unnecessary infrastructure. Each layer of complexity introduces additional demands, resource management challenges, and escalated costs. While the inclination may be to augment complexity with workarounds, urging employees to simplify and diminish complexity presents a more substantial challenge. Nevertheless, the advantages of streamlining processes far surpass the additional effort involved.

Be intentional in all aspects of what is introduced and institutionalized as corporate infrastructure. Make conscious decisions about what enters the organization and what is left behind. Uncluttering organizational spaces will not only liberate physical areas but also elevate the energy of associates as they contend with less to manage. There is a tendency to perpetually accumulate and retain processes and legacy systems far beyond their optimal duration. Adopting a mindset that appreciates both addition and subtraction in the pursuit of improvement can lead to outcomes that are not only more efficient but also more cost-effective.

Establishing a structured process not only instills organization but also fosters stability and strategic thinking. It serves as a powerful tool in eliminating the noise of busy work and menial tasks, allowing individuals to dedicate focused time to strategic considerations. In contrast, the absence of a well-defined process can plunge an environment into chaos, compelling employees to constantly engage in firefighting and improvisation to navigate numerous unknowns.

Consider the analogy of storing dishes and silverware in different locations after each meal. The ensuing disarray would transform every future meal preparation into a time-consuming exercise of searching for essential items before even starting. The chaos created by the lack of organization would overshadow the enjoyment of the meal. Strikingly, a parallel situation unfolds in our professional lives, where a barrage of instructions through numerous communication channels creates a scavenger hunt, making it challenging to piece together and understand our responsibilities.

This scattered communication approach resembles a business version of storing items in different places each time, leading to genuine confusion when recipients struggle to decipher the intended message. The natural consequence is that outcomes fall short of expectations. Embracing a structured process can not only enhance efficiency but also contribute to a more harmonious and productive work environment.

Your continuous improvement journey begins by hitting the pause button and engaging in thoughtful reflection on both the positive and negative aspects of the organization. While relying on data is crucial, questioning the data and its origins is equally important. Asking the right questions is more valuable than simply trying to generate solutions. Invite leaders to actively listen to their employees, decoding the messages they are trying to convey. It's essential to go beyond the surface and uncover the "secret" conversations and storytelling that harbor genuine truths about the organizational culture. By tapping into these authentic dialogues, leaders can extract valuable insights and apply their employees' collective wisdom to unlock the organization's full potential. This process not only fosters a more cohesive and informed workplace but also sets the stage for addressing challenges and implementing positive changes based on a deeper understanding of the organization's dynamics.

Acknowledgments

Over the past decades, I have had the privilege of collaborating with hundreds of associates who generously shared their stories, insights, and epiphanies—each contribution forming the foundation for this book.

I express my deepest gratitude to Dave Ellingen, whose tenure as president of Mitchell1 and Snap-on Diagnostics granted me unprecedented access to both organizations. This access—extending from facilities to senior management—allowed me to immerse myself in the intricacies of the businesses and learn side by side with the employees. I consider myself the smartest woman in the organization, not due to my education, but because I was uniquely positioned to create and review daily our problem-solving library of thousands of individual and team projects. The wisdom I gained is nearly impossible to replicate. In speaking to others globally, I have come to appreciate the gift my career trajectory has given me.

I extend a special acknowledgment to Professor Lenny Perry from the University of San Diego, whose role in launching and guiding my journey has been instrumental. His exceptional ability to convey complex concepts with clarity and vivid examples revealed to me the transformative power of storytelling in teaching the principles of process excellence. Professor Perry's current position in the AME San Diego Consortium has provided me with an opportunity to engage with other continuous improvement (CI) professionals in my local area at a deeper level.

Thanks to Lenny and the Consortium, I have gained a deeper understanding of the critical role that interaction with fellow professionals plays in my ongoing professional growth. Actively participating in various global organizations has become a key aspect of my approach, ensuring I continuously seek diverse perspectives from professionals across different regions. This commitment to engaging with a broad network has significantly enriched my understanding and contributed to my ongoing development in the field.

My sincere thanks to Ozzie Gontang, my executive coach and endless cheerleader. In moments when guidance was crucial, Ozzie introduced me to Toni Davies, whose counsel laid the foundation for our company's transformative journey. Toni's remarkable expertise and firsthand experiences with Japanese sensei and world-class organizations have proven to be an invaluable resource. Her generosity in sharing her knowledge, coupled with her kindness, played a pivotal role in crafting the blueprint for our organization. I am truly thankful for the guidance and insights that Ozzie and Toni have brought to our journey of transformation.

As for Ozzie, I am unsure what would have become of my career without his guidance. Thank you for recognizing my skills and abilities and refining my rough edges and communication style. Being right is useless if you can't influence and move the organization in the right direction. Thank you for teaching me the power of coaching and empowering people.

A special thank you to Susan Scott, whose book and workshops taught me the most powerful statement: "The conversation is the relationship." Her influence, stemming from my days at Vistage International, significantly shaped my coaching style and emphasized the importance of coaching individuals rather than imposing rigid methodologies.

A heartfelt thank you to my family for being patient and providing unwavering support when work took me away from home. Thank you to my children Paulina, Bella, and Aaron and their infinite understanding of my demanding schedule.

To all my incredible friends who constantly encouraged me to finish the project, a big hug and thank you for all your love and support. To Mike, Toan, Abel, Anton, Alfonso, Brad, and Cecy, your encouragement propelled me from talking about writing to actually writing.

About The Author

Maribel Topf, a proud San Diego native and first-generation American, embarked on her academic journey at Stephens College, humorously dubbing it "Steve's School for Chicks." This moniker resonates with the incredible women she encountered during her college years and her subsequent professional endeavors in male-dominated industries. Maribel often joked the potential title for her first book would be "*The Only Woman in the Room*."

Her upbringing in a Spanish-speaking household, coupled with attending college in the Midwest, constituted a profound and transformative experience. Discovering the warmth of a Latin family within the context of Midwestern women and values altered her perceptions of what a modern woman could be. Embracing the role of supporting women while learning from the amazing men she encountered throughout her career has deepened Maribel's respect for the challenges inherent in both life and professional pursuits for both genders. Her journey reflects a harmonious integration of diverse perspectives, fostering a rich understanding of the shared struggles and triumphs we all encounter.

Maribel has dedicated a significant portion of her career to collaborating with the C-suite. From her contributions at Vistage, a CEO membership organization, to her nearly two decades in the Repair Information & Diagnostics divisions of Snap-on, she has played a pivotal role in assisting executives in translating their strategies and visions into actionable plans at the employee level. Over the last twelve years, Maribel has successfully managed the continuous improvement programs for two companies, overseeing the progress of almost 1,000 employees. Her strategic leadership has made these companies some of the most profitable within the Snap-on family of companies. Throughout her tenure, she has reviewed and overseen an impressive portfolio of over 10,000 employee-led continuous improvement projects, further solidifying her reputation as a key driver of organizational success.

With an affinity for the diverse and unconventional in life, literature, and friendships, Maribel constantly seeks out unique experiences. During her free time, she immerses herself in the most eclectic events, exploring everything her city and travel adventures have to offer. Proud of her Oaxacan heritage, she finds solace in her home away from home whenever possible, indulging in a well-deserved shot or two of Mezcal to reconnect with her roots.

Endnotes

[1] A.V. Feigenbaum, *Total Quality Control*, 3rd ed. (New York: McGraw-Hill, 1991).

[2] Thomas Psyzdek, *The Six Sigma Handbook*, (New York: McGraw-Hill, 2003).

[3] Matthew Panzarino, "How Pixar's Toy Story 2 Was Deleted Twice, Once By Technology, and Again for Its Own Good," *TNW Newsletter*, May 21, 2012, https://thenextweb.com/news/how-pixars-toy-story-2-was-deleted-twice-once-by-technology-and-again-for-its-own-good.

[4] Daniel Kahneman, *Thinking, Fast and Slow*, (Toronto: Doubleday Canada, 2011).

[5] Umar Tahir, "Nudge Management in Change Theory," *Change Management Insight*, January 18, 2020, https://changemanagementinsight.com/nudge-theory-in-change-management/

[6] Paul A. Akers, *2 Second Lean* (Ferndale, WA: FastCap Press, 2014).

[7] John J. Gabarro, "When A New Manager Takes Charge," *Harvard Business Review*, January 2007, https://hbr.org/2007/01/when-a-new-manager-takes-charge.

[8] "Guide: Understand Team Effectiveness," *re: Work* (blog), Google, accessed September 7, 2023. https://rework.withgoogle.com/print/guides/5721312655835136/

[9] Brigid Schulte, "Work interruptions can cost you 6 hours a day. An efficiency expert explains how to avoid them," *The Washington Post*, June 1, 2015, https://www.washingtonpost.com/news/inspired-life/wp/2015/06/01/interruptions-at-work-can-cost-you-up-to-6-hours-a-day-heres-how-to-avoid-them/

[10] "Why Multi-tasking Doesn't Work," Cleveland Clinic, March 10, 2021, https://health.clevelandclinic.org/science-clear-multitasking-doesnt-work

[11] "New Measure of Human Brain Processing Speed," *MIT Technology Review*, August 25, 2009, https://www.technologyreview.com/2009/08/25/210267/new-measure-of-human-brain-processing-speed/

[12] Paige Bennett, "15 Start-up Newsletters for Entrepreneurs," *Hubspot for Start-ups*, September 9, 2023, https://blog.hubspot.com/the-hustle/startup-newsletter

[13] Tony McCafferty, "Brain Swarming: A New Approach to Finding Solutions", O'Reilly.com, Accessed December 20, 2023, https://www.oreilly.com/library/view/hbr-guide-to/9781633698161/Text/15_6_BrainSwarming__A_New_Approach.html

[14] Richard Koch, *The 80/20 Principle*, (New York: Doubleday, 1998)

[15] Malcolm Gladwell, *The Bomber Mafia*, (Boston: Little, Brown and Co., 2021).

[16] Nir Eyal, *Indistractable*, (Dallas: Benbella Books, 2019).

[17] Alex Hern, "Myspace Loses All Content Uploaded Before 2016," *The Guardian*, May 18, 2019, https://www.theguardian.com/technology/2019/mar/18/myspace-loses-all-content-uploaded-before-2016

[18] Kasey Panetta, "Gartner's Top 10 Security Predictions 2016," Gartner.com, June 15, 2016, https://www.gartner.com/smarterwithgartner/top-10-security-predictions-2016?cm_mmc=social-_rm-_-gart-_-swa

[19] Jason M. Watson and David L. Strayer, "Supertaskers: Profiles in extraordinary multitasking ability," *Psychonomic Bulletin and Review*, August 2010, https://link.springer.com/article/10.3758/PBR.17.4.479

[20] Ryuji Fukuda, *Building Organizational Fitness: Management Methodology for Transformation and Strategic Advantage*, 1st ed. (Danvers, MA: Productivity Press, 1997).

[21] Carol Dweck, *Mindset: New Psychology of Success*, (New York: Ballantine Books, 2013). (PAGE 98)

www.ingramcontent.com/pod-product-compliance
Lightning Source LLC
Chambersburg PA
CBHW031941190326
41519CB00007B/603